Daniel Im is one of our generation's [...] thinkers, one of God's gifts to the [...] a culture that is transfixed with the [...] selves, this book offers a different alternative—one rooted in the imago dei and the gospel. This is a helpful, thoughtful, inspiring book with a timely message.

—J.D. Greear, pastor, The Summit Church, Durham, North Carolina, and author of *Above All*

This book will hit close to home. Daniel Im's incisive cultural analysis is more than a big-picture overview of massive structural shifts. It's an unflinching look at the way those shifts have changed our perception of ourselves, the world, and God. And his answer to these shifts is, thankfully, full of grace and truth. *You Are What You Do* is both a brutal excavation of our deepest assumptions and a healing balm for what ails us. I needed this book, and it came at just the right moment.

—Richard Clark, podcast producer, host, and manager with *Christianity Today*

Hustling . . . side gigging . . . cross-fitting? Finding meaning in what you do or own or who you know? Minus the cross-fitting, this book felt like it was written just for me. Resist the lies and follow Christ. Daniel Im nailed it in *You Are What You Do: And Six Other Lies About Work, Life, and Love.*

—Scarlet Hiltibidal, author of *Afraid of All the Things*

While these lies might seem harmless, I've seen the destruction and chaos that ensues when you live according to them.

So do yourself a favor and read this book—not just for your sake, but for the health of everyone around you.

—Ed Stetzer, Wheaton College

In this book Daniel Im gives us a helpful and timely reminder of the joy that comes from living in response to already being approved, already belonging, and already being loved because of the good news of Jesus. We don't have to achieve our identity; we can happily receive from the only One who can truly satisfy us.

—Eric Geiger, senior pastor Mariners Church

It's not just technology and culture that's changing, technology and culture are changing us too. In *You Are What You Do*, Daniel Im unpacks some important lies about who we are, our true identity and where our value comes from. Getting the truth right now is one of the most important things you can do to get ready for the future.

—Carey Nieuwhof, founding pastor, Connexus Church
and author of *Didn't See It Coming*

The natural inclination of the human heart is to seek meaning, purpose, and identity in ways that diminish us more than they build us up. For some of us, we look for identity in our work. For others of us, it's our relationships, our knowledge, our experiences, our good name, or any number of other things. In each instance, and as the old adage goes, we are "barking up the wrong tree." In the end, none of these things will deliver on the promises they make to us. Meanwhile, the Lord says to us, "Come to me, all you who are weary and burdened, and I will give you rest." And it is from that place of rest that he heals us with reminders that his love is fixed, that there is nothing we can do to lose it, and our identity is that of beloved daughters and sons. It turns out, as Daniel reminds us so effectively in this book, that we aren't what we do. Rather, we are who God says we are, and that is more than enough.

—Scott Sauls, senior pastor of Christ Presbyterian Church and author of several books, including *Jesus Outside the Lines* and *Irresistible Faith*

You Are What You Do: And Six Other Lies about Work, Life, and Love is a bold book that powerfully tells you the truth about yourself. Daniel Im has identified the most common lies we tell ourselves, explains the unspeakable damage they do and counters them with the truth that God speaks to us. If you have ever felt defeated, stuck, or afraid—this book can set you free!

—Dave Ferguson, author of *Hero Maker: Five Essential Practices for Leaders to Multiply Leaders*

Daniel's writing is an important message for anyone who is struggling to identify where their worth comes from. In a culture that places so much importance on productivity, experience, and success, Im reminds us that our identity is found in Jesus' life giving sacrifice on the cross. That's a message I'll never get tired of hearing!

—Jonathan JP Pokluda, author of *Welcome to Adulting* and lead pastor of Harris Creek in Waco, TX

Daniel has penned a unique view of the world and some of our common responses to it. In doing so, he exposes some lies which can easily distract all of us and then helps us with a proper and biblical perspective to address them. This book is a much needed pause and a reminder of what matters most in life. I highly recommend it.

—Ron Edmondson, CEO, Leadership Network
and author of *The Mythical Leader*

Daniel Im's newest book, *You Are What You Do*, is a powerful tool for addressing how today's complex society can leave us misdirected, unfulfilled, and shamed—even when we appear successful! Weaving together current research, personal vulnerability and fresh insights from Scripture, I found this a refreshing and hopeful message for all generations. I will be handing this book out A LOT!

—Kadi Cole, leadership consultant, executive coach,
and author of *Developing Female Leaders*

YOU ARE WHAT YOU DO

AND SIX OTHER LIES ABOUT WORK, LIFE, & LOVE

DANIEL IM

B&H
PUBLISHING
NASHVILLE, TENNESSEE

To Christina, thank you for being the first one
to remind me that I am not what I do.

Acknowledgments

I am not a self-made man. There's not one single accomplishment that I can take 100 percent of the credit for. In fact, if it weren't for the people that I'm about to acknowledge, this book wouldn't be what it is. So here's my attempt at tracing the threads of this book back to the people who have most directly influenced it.

To Taylor Combs and Devin Maddox, thank you for nudging me to write this book. If you hadn't sent me that text message after listening to my talk on the gig economy a couple years ago in Atlanta, I would have never even thought to tackle a project like this. Taylor, thank you for helping shape this book into what it is and for caring about this book as much as me—you're legit bro. And to the incredible team at B&H Publishing, thank you for believing in me and for your partnership on this book. You're proof that there is no such thing as a solo author.

To everyone who listened to my early musings about this book, thank you. Jeremy Maxfield, when are you going to realize that God is calling you to Canada to serve with me? Dave Schroeder, I don't know if I've ever met a nicer 'Merican. Todd Adkins, I miss our white board sessions. Kevin Peck, thanks for taking a random call from some Canadian almost a decade ago. And Ed Stetzer, despite the fact that you never gave me that luggage back, you're incredibly generous as a leader, mentor, and friend.

To LifeWay, The Fellowship, and all our friends back in Mt. Juliet and Nashville, boy do we ever miss y'all. This book was birthed out of the context of ministering and doing life with you. So thank you! If you ever want to visit the Canadian Rockies and experience a real winter where milk, bread, and eggs don't fly off the shelves at the threat of snow, look us up. We'd love to host you!

To the staff and congregation of Beulah, did you ever think that my visit back in January 2019 would be the catalyst that God would use to bring us back? God is writing an incredible story in Edmonton and we're just getting started. So buckle up because 1 percent is just the starting point! Christina and I love you and we're praying for you daily.

Thank you Appa and Umma for your constant love, investment, guidance, and prayers. The goodness of God and His everlasting love are incredibly tangible for me to grasp because of your example.

To Victoria, Adelyn, and Makarios, thank you for sacrificing big breakfast on Saturday mornings so that Daddy could write this book. I want you to know that God used the three of you to shape the ideas in this book. And not only do your mommy and I consider it an honor and privilege to be your parents, but we're incredibly grateful for the ways that God uses y'all to continue to refine and shape us.

To Christina, thank you for your conviction surrounding this book and in its importance. Thank you for believing in me, for creating the space so that I could write, and for encouraging me to keep on going even when I was ready to give up. Enneagram 3s unite!

And finally to my Lord and Savior Jesus Christ. This book would be pointless if you hadn't done what you did. Thank you for offering us a better narrative and life than anything out there. You are not just a way or a truth in the midst of this thing we call life. No, you are The Way, The Truth, and The Life. Thank you for never giving up on us.

Contents

Introduction

I f there's anything constant in life, it's change.

Just consider how commonplace cauliflower, podcasting, and Amazon Prime have become—and how quickly it's happened. Growing up, no one ever talked about cauliflower, let alone wanted to eat the tasteless and smelly thing. Yet recently, you've probably tried (or heard of) cauliflower rice, cauliflower pizza crust, cauliflower buffalo wings, or cauliflower tots. And if you haven't, your friends have. Now just to give you a sense of its meteoric rise, in a short span of three years, Green Giant has gone from harvesting five to thirty acres of cauliflower *each* week. That's 100,000 heads of cauliflower every single day![1] And they are just one of the many companies that have hopped on the cauliflower bandwagon.[2]

A similar thing has happened with podcasting. When I started listening to podcasts in 2008, it was a multistep process that required a computer. Today, however, with the ubiquity of smartphones, listening to podcasts has become so commonplace and normal that the question has shifted from "Have you heard of podcasts?" to "Which podcasts do you listen to?" In fact, in the last five years, close to half of all Americans and Canadians tuned into their first podcast episode.[3]

And let's not forget the explosive growth of Amazon Prime.[4] Now that more than half of all American households are subscribing members, isn't it odd to meet someone who doesn't have it? It's definitely become the exception, rather than the norm.

Imagine going to the grocery store and *half* of the produce was rotten. Would you notice? If you were driving home from work, would you notice if *half* of the cars were off the road? And what if you ordered a burger from your favorite restaurant and *half* of it was missing? By the time something reaches the 50 percent mark, wouldn't you have to be living in a hole to miss it? Unfortunately though, noticing doesn't necessarily lead to action.

Noticing the negative grade around your house doesn't necessarily mean that you'll fix it right away. Seeing the check engine light go off doesn't necessarily mean you'll drop everything and take your car into the shop. And realizing that your pants are fitting tighter than before doesn't mean that you'll immediately go on a diet.

Moments of change happen when things shift from being *a* problem to being *my* problem. These are the moments we transform into action mode—moments when we find water in our basement, are stuck on the side of the road, or realize that nothing we have fits anymore.

While this might be true for the things that are happening *to* you, what about all the change that is happening *around* you—around us in society today? With trends like the ones mentioned above, rising and falling so rapidly, is there a way to tell the difference between fads and fundamentals? Between the passing and permanent? Between fidget spinners and artificial intelligence?

Things Have Changed

When I moved to Nashville in 2014, I noticed something. I didn't realize how critical of a trend it was going to become, the extent that it was going to impact everyday life, the rapid rate at which it was growing, or how it was going to become the new normal, but it seemed like everyone had a side hustle or a gig. Okay, maybe not *everyone*, but close to half of the people I met. And for the majority of them, these gigs weren't their main source of income—a lot of them were hustling, contracting, and moonlighting on the side to earn some extra cash, pay down debt, or save up for a vacation.

It was kind of like cauliflower, podcasting, and Amazon Prime—no matter where you went, it was hard to miss. Heck, even I was a part of this trend with all the writing, podcasting, consulting, and speaking I was doing on the side.

At first, I thought this was an American thing, since I had just moved to the States, but after talking to friends in Canada, reflecting back on the time my wife and I lived in Korea, and doing some research, I quickly realized how much of a global trend this was becoming—and how rapidly it was growing.[5]

While there's no consensus on what to call this new normal—gigging, freelancing, contracting, side hustling, moonlighting—the important thing is to know what it is and how it's affecting you because it's here to stay. Some experts refer to it as the gig economy, but don't let that scare you. It's just a label. This isn't a book on finances, economics, blockchain, or getting rich off of cryptocurrency—it's actually quite the opposite.

As long as you haven't cloistered yourself off from the rest of the world in an isolated "off-the-grid" commune where you're stuck in time and nothing ever changes, you will find this book helpful. Just think of it as a pair of glasses that will bring this new normal into focus, so that you can see all the subversive ways that it's trying to change the way you approach work, life, and love.

Do You See It?

My wife, Christina, sees it. After all, she's living it every day. In addition to being a full-time mom to our three children, she runs point on our podcast and works as an independent contractor doing content marketing.

When I was speaking at a conference in Vancouver, my hometown, the grad student who drove me around saw it as well. In addition to school and a full-time job, he had a side hustle doing wedding photography on the weekends.

All of the Uber drivers I meet see it as well. Especially the retired educator who recently drove me to the airport while I was on my way to speak at a conference in Orange County. After only one month of retirement, he was back at it.

Most of my friends see it too. Some have quit their full-time job, with guaranteed salary and benefits, to start their own thing. Others have started their own thing on the side, in hopes that it will one day replace their full-time job. And the rest—who are the majority—don't plan on leaving their nine-to-five job with benefits and paid vacation anytime soon. They just have a side hustle to help pay down debt, go on vacation, do home improvements, or simply afford the rising cost of life. It's become the new credit card.

Do you see how things have changed? Just working a steady nine-to-five job is not normal anymore. Having a single source of income is definitely not normal either.

And these days, waiting until you're retired to explore the world, try new experiences, eat delicious food, and enjoy life certainly does not fit into anyone's definition of normal—if retirement is even a thing anymore. What's normal is a desire for freedom and flexibility, which conveniently is exactly what the gig economy promises.

And contrary to common belief, this is not just something that affects those in their twenties and thirties. According to the research, people in every generation are gigging because this desire for freedom and flexibility has become our new oxygen.[6] It's the air we breathe and the water we drink. In fact, it's become so commonplace that it's no longer the exception.

The Gig Economy *Is* the New Normal

In 2018, 35 percent of the American workforce was a part of the gig economy—up from five years prior. That means 56.7 million Americans were self-employed in a part-time or full-time capacity getting paid for their time, skills, possessions, or expertise. To give you some perspective, that's more people than the entire populations of Canada, Liberia, Greece, and Puerto Rico combined! And what's so surprising about it all is just how rapidly the gig economy has grown. Can you believe that 74 percent of all gig workers surveyed joined the gig economy in the last five years?[7]

You see similar trends in Canada, the United Kingdom, and Australia, where the growing gig economy continues to affect normal everyday work, life, and love.[8] In fact, if you were to look up "gig economy" in Google Trends, you would see an upward trend in search relevance beginning July 2015.[9] And this is not just in the United States, Canada, United Kingdom, or Australia. You see this globally, with Singapore topping the list.

The gig economy has quickly become the new normal because of the way that it's changing everyday life. You don't even need to be working in it for it to affect you. Just think about the last time you bought something off of Facebook Marketplace, rode in an Uber, ordered food using Grubhub, slept at an Airbnb, or got your IKEA furniture assembled by a Tasker from TaskRabbit. That was all possible thanks to the gig economy and someone else's side hustle.

The same is true even without an app, because every time you get a haircut, hire a contractor, have your lawn mowed, or hire a babysitter, you are also funding the gig economy.

Like the rise of cauliflower, podcasting, and Amazon Prime, the gig economy has followed suit—it's become the new normal. The major difference is that unlike cauliflower, podcasting, and Amazon Prime, this change is not only happening *around* you, it's happening *to* you. And it's not as harmless as you might initially think.

Leeches, Lies, and Loose Threads

While I was researching the implications of the gig economy on everyday life, I noticed a loose thread. Initially, I ignored it, thinking that it was probably nothing. But the longer I spent investigating how the gig economy affected everyday life, the more the loose thread seemed to stick out.

It kept jeering and taunting me to pull it. So I did. And that's when things began to unravel. The glitz and glamor of the gig economy came undone the more I pulled. Stitch after stitch loosened and fell apart, until I was eventually left with a mangled heap of lies:

You are what you do.

You are what you experience.

You are who you know.

You are what you know.

You are what you own.

You are who you raise.

You are your past.

I couldn't believe all the subtle and subversive ways that the lies of the gig economy were trying to change the way I approached work, life, and love. It reminded me of a leech.

Leeches have been used for thousands of years medicinally—and while there are still some doctors today that will use them to help heal skin grafts, let's be honest, they're nasty.[10] They always have been and they always will be. They're predatory, parasitic, and just downright disgusting. If it wasn't bad enough that you can't feel them when they latch onto you, if you remove them incorrectly, they can actually regurgitate bacteria-filled blood from their gut into your wound. If you get too many bites, then your body can lose its ability to clot blood. And if the leech gets into your body . . . I can't even finish the sentence, it's so gross.[11]

Well, just like the three-jawed mouth of a leech that subtly latches itself onto you when swimming in a lake—without you even feeling it—these lies have done the same. They have released an anesthetic, like a leech does when it starts sucking your blood, so that you don't notice them nor feel them until they've finished what they started. That is, until they've changed the way that you define yourself, judge your self-worth, and seek contentment in life.

Here's the thing. Though I'm getting the heebie-jeebies just writing this, leeches aren't *that* bad, because they can't touch your soul—they can't get inside of you like these lies can (and probably already have). While you might be able to see some of the ways that these lies are already directing your life on the surface, the scary thing is that the other lies are also there—they're just lurking underneath, lying dormant until an opportune time.

So just like we can't eradicate leeches from lakes or forests, these seven lies are the same—they're just there, whether we like it or not. We can't get rid of them, so we have to figure out a way to deal with them.

No wonder leeches are written about in the Bible like this: "A leech has twin daughters named 'Gimme' and 'Gimme more'" (Prov. 30:15 MSG). What an apt description for these seven lies! They're demanding, relentless, and taxing our souls and lives in ways that most of us can't even begin to comprehend.

I wonder if the apostle Paul had experience with similar kinds of lies (or leeches) in his day, because he seems to know how to deal with them: "Do not be conformed to this age, but be transformed by the renewing of your mind, so that you may discern what is the good, pleasing, and perfect will of God" (Rom. 12:2).

Instead of conforming to the lies of our age by accepting them without thinking twice, what if we resisted? And by resistance, I'm not talking about passively ignoring them, I'm talking about the kind of active resistance that the apostle Paul talks about—the kind of resistance that seeks to uncover the truth at all costs, no matter how much it might hurt.

This is the kind of resistance that chooses love over hate, light over darkness, forgiveness over shame, and generosity over greed. It's the kind of resistance that uncovers who we aren't, so that we can begin the journey of discovering who we really are. And this kind of resistance begins here with the truth that you are not what you do, you are not what you experience, you are not who you know, you are not what you know, you are not what you own, you are not who you raise, and you are not your past.

Conclusion

Before Airbnb was even a thing, my mom had it figured out. Not only was our basement always rented out, but so was every spare room in our house. It was a silver bullet—if there ever was such a thing—because she would rent out the rooms to the constant stream of international students from Korea.

It was genius, and that was just a side hustle. My parents also started a string of businesses, culminating in a billiard hall, thanks to which my dad would come home at 2:00 a.m. every morning smelling like smoke.

They were the originals of the gig economy before it was even called the gig economy.

Maybe it's because my mom grew up on a farm or because my dad was born during the Korean War. Or it could be that they learned it when leaving everything in Korea to immigrate to Canada. Or perhaps, it's just because they had four children and had to make ends meet. Whatever the case, they lived it, they modeled it, and they raised my sisters and I to do the same.

It was in the air we breathed and the water we drank. For us, gigging and hustling was normal—we had no other choice. It was an issue of survival for my family.

Here's why I'm telling you all of this. It's because today *this is* the new normal. Hustling is not just for immigrants anymore; it's for everyone. And that's why I wrote this book.

I didn't write it to give you seven steps to a better life. Or, for you to learn how to crack some code, get rich quick, work a four-hour workweek, or unlock hidden secrets about yourself. I'm not going to guilt or shame you. I'm not just going to tell you to work harder either. And I'm definitely not offering you productivity hacks so that you can get more done.

Instead, I want to show you the subtle ways that this new normal—the gig economy—has changed everyday life through the lies that it has ushered in. Then and only then will we be able to do something about it, so that we can move from passivity to action. From surviving to thriving.

Chapter 1

Hustle

Blank stare. Tossed hair. And a longing to be elsewhere.

If you're up for it, let's play a game of "Guess Who?" It's simple. Just try and guess who I'm looking at right now.

Hangry, irritable, and unable to focus.

Is a picture of someone forming in your mind? Here are a few more descriptors.

Piles of dirty laundry, protein bar wrappers in the trash, and a cup of coffee that's been warmed up one too many times.

If you guessed a prisoner, an executive, or a working parent, you're close, but not quite there yet. If you guessed yourself, you're closer, but that probably means one of two things—you're either sleep deprived or a doer.

Recently, one of the largest online marketplaces for freelancers ran an ad campaign in New York subways plastering up headshots of doers and excerpts from their interviews. They called this campaign "The Year of Do," with the catchy tag line, "In Doers We Trust."[1]

Here's the excerpt from the ad I'm looking at: "You eat a coffee for lunch. You follow through on your follow through. Sleep deprivation is your drug of choice. You might be a doer."[2]

Apparently doing has become a badge of honor. A status symbol. And *the way* to define ourselves.

Freedom and Flexibility

When traveling, one of my favorite things to do is talk to my Uber driver. I've been driven around by college students, graduate students, cyber security analysts, insurance agents, retired veterans, full-time moms, an HOA president, and a guy in finance who had just lost his job because his CEO and CFO went to prison. Although they all have different reasons for driving, a common theme I've heard over and over again is a desire for freedom and flexibility—regardless of age, ethnicity, and whether they were doing it part-time or full-time. Since freedom and flexibility are hallmarks of the gig economy, this makes complete sense.

One of my favorite conversations was with a fifty-something full-time mother, who for the first time in thirty years was earning a paycheck outside of the home. Since she could drive whenever she wanted to, Uber was a perfect fit for her to earn "spending money." So several nights a week from 9:00 p.m. to 1:00 a.m.—since by that time everything has settled down at home—she gets in her car, opens up the app, and starts her side hustle.

I remember this other conversation I had with Melissa, a single mom who, after putting in a full day as a cleaner, would drive for Uber in the evenings and weekends to support her three teenagers. Her dream is to start her own cleaning company one day, but in the meantime, driving an extra twenty hours a week does the trick to pay for those "dang expensive pizza pockets," in her words.

Teenagers eat a lot of food—and one pizza pocket isn't enough to fill a growing adolescent after school. I get that, since that was me as a teenager. But I remember, even after eating a pizza pocket or two, I'd still be hungry for dinner a couple hours later! Well, it's the same for Melissa's children—the only problem is that now, pizza pockets cost a lot more! In fact, everything costs more. So for Melissa, working an extra twenty hours a week is the only means she has to afford those pizza pockets and chip away at her credit card debt, while also saving up for that upcoming trip to Atlanta.

I could go on and on and tell you about the number of dads I met who were driving for Uber, as a side hustle, to pay for extra expenses. Others were driving to save up for their children's college tuition. And still others would rather earn some extra spending cash than relax with their family on the weekend.

I've even met individuals who see their side hustle as the new credit card. Instead of going into debt to go on vacation, they just gig a few hours a week to save up. This is the new normal.

Let's get back to the "Guess Who?" game. It'd be one thing if the lady on this poster looked happy, but she doesn't. Sure, by doing more—or gigging—she might have earned some extra cash, but was it worth it? She looks miserable, scattered, anxious, dehydrated, and emotionless.

If this is the end result of doing, I don't want it. It doesn't look like much of a status symbol to me. In doers, I *don't* want to trust.

Lie #1: You Are What You Do

A couple years after getting married, Christina and I moved to Korea. Until then, though we had visited other countries, neither of us had ever lived outside of Canada. In fact, we were about to purchase our first home in Montreal, but when I got a job offer to work at one of the largest churches in the world—I'm not exaggerating, it was a church of fifty thousand people—our priorities conveniently changed in an instant.

"Isn't this a once-in-a-lifetime sort of opportunity? I'd be stupid to say no, right? After all, we don't even have children yet. This would skyrocket my career. Just imagine what this would look like on my résumé! God has to be in this, otherwise, why else would I get such an opportunity? I'm going to make such a greater impact there than I would here, so isn't this a no-brainer?"

I've forgotten which of those phrases I said to Christina, which ones I kept hidden in my heart, and which ones I wasn't even aware of myself, but that paragraph pretty much sums it up—and I'm not proud of it.

Within a couple months, we sold everything—including my beloved Volkswagen GTI—packed what we could in a few suitcases, stored what we could at Christina's parents' place, and bought a one-way ticket to Seoul, South Korea.

The plan was to stay there long-term. Christina enrolled in Korean lessons, was working with me at the church, and started her masters in counseling. I was pastoring, finishing up graduate school, and teaching English on the side. Life was good and things were fruitful. In fact, they were so fruitful that a year after we moved to Korea, we became a family of three! So with our baby girl, we decided it was time to grow up and move out of our furnished apartment in the party district. We wanted to lay down roots, so we found a nice little two-bedroom apartment and furnished it ourselves. We even bought an oven, which wasn't a normal appliance for a typical Korean home. Can you tell momma bird was nesting?

Life was really good, until everything started to unravel. And by everything, this time I really do mean *everything*. A few months after moving into our new apartment, we lost our jobs, our closest friends, and our home. We lost our livelihood and everything was taken out from under our feet. In short, my ladder-climbing-résumé-building-career-rocketing adventure abruptly came to an end, and we had to move back to Canada.

I was devastated.

Once the dust settled, I started wondering if we had somehow made the wrong decision. Maybe we were never supposed to go in the first place. Perhaps I incorrectly assumed that God was leading us (because of my mixed motives), when in fact, it was just a good opportunity.

I was also ashamed.

What would I say to the doubters who thought we were making a mistake to sell everything and move halfway across the world? What would I say to my parents who were leery of us going in the first place? How was I supposed to support my wife and child now that I was without a job and essentially homeless? And why did I feel like someone had just punched me in the gut, stolen my keys, and driven off with my car? After all, it's just a job, isn't it?

What Do You Do for Work?

As children, we're asked what we want to do when we grow up. As adults, we're asked what we do for work. And at the end of our lives, we're measured by what we've done. It's not surprising, then, that we believe the lie that we *are* what we *do*. It seems to be the primary way that we ascribe value and worth onto one another—and ourselves.

If you remember telling your parents that you wanted to be an artist, musician, or athlete when you grew up, you probably learned from an early age that not all jobs are created equal. What's up with that? Who made the decision that becoming an engineer, lawyer, or doctor was fundamentally better than being a creative anyway? And what does "better" even mean? Just more money? And why do parents feel like it's their universal responsibility to set their kids straight and teach them this *proper* hierarchy of jobs?

Referencing an article in *The New York Times*, Timothy Keller put it well:

> So many college students do not choose work that actually fits their abilities, talents, and capacities, but rather choose work

that fits within their limited imagination of how they can boost their own self-image. There were only three high-status kinds of jobs—those that paid well, those that directly worked on society's needs, and those that had the cool factor. Because there is no longer an operative consensus on the dignity of all work, still less on the idea that in all work we are the hands and fingers of God serving the human community, in their minds they had an extremely limited range of career choices. That means lots of young adults are choosing work that doesn't fit them, or fields that are too highly competitive for most people to do well in. And this sets many people up for a sense of dissatisfaction or meaninglessness in their work.[3]

No wonder we over-identify ourselves with our jobs—we've been conditioned to do so, both from within and from without. So to satisfy both our internal craving for meaning and our external drive for a particular quality of life, we look for the perfect job. A job that boosts our self-image and also pays the bills. And if the latter is lacking, no worries—that's why the gig economy exists. An extra gig here or side hustle there never hurt anyone, right?

Pressure, Platforms, and Pretending

What happens when our being is defined by our doing? When we believe the lie that we are what we do? And when this becomes the primary lens through which we measure success?

Pressure

Wouldn't you feel an enormous amount of pressure to do more so that you can get more, have more, and be more? Unfortunately, this is a never-ending cycle because there's always more to do. It's kind of like laundry—it never ends. And even when you think you've done enough, there are always others who have accomplished more than you, which then leads to even more pressure to do more.

Platform

In today's world, in order to do bigger and better things, don't you have to have a platform? If people don't know what you're doing, are you really doing it? While platforms in and of themselves are neutral, the problem is that they often open the door to a compartmentalized life. This leads to a separation between the private and public, and as it grows over the years, fewer people are let in on the inside, until eventually you've locked everyone out—including yourself. Now to be clear, this doesn't have to happen, but unfortunately, it's often what does. Isn't that why it was so shocking to hear of Robin Williams's, Anthony Bourdain's, and Kate Spade's suicides? Weren't they finally enjoying the benefits of all they'd done?

Pretend

If you can't keep up with the pressure, and building a platform isn't going as well as you thought, isn't the next best option just to pretend? Fake it 'til you make it, right? Buy followers on social media, pay people to purchase your products, and pad your numbers. If it worked for some of the most recent start-ups, why wouldn't it work for you? Just listen to the podcast, *How I Built This,* and you'll see how many hacked their way to success.

Unfortunately, the thing about pretending is that it always leads to anxiety. You're constantly looking over your shoulder, wondering when you'll be found out, and what will happen then.

A life dictated by doing is not much of a life at all. How many more executives, entrepreneurs, and spiritual leaders need to lose their families, and their own souls, for us to get it? And how many more public personalities need to implode before we learn from their mistakes and pivot? When we let this lie define our lives, we inevitably end up neglecting the relationships that mean the most to us, our emotional well-being, and our spiritual health. Isn't that why we're called human *be*ings, and not human *do*ings?

~~You Are What You Do~~

When we arrived back to Canada, we moved in with my parents. With no job, no purpose, and nowhere to go, they graciously let us stay in their house until we could get back on our feet.

I was resolved to move out as soon as I could—not because I didn't love my parents, but because I was a married man with a child. So instead of bumming around in my Pj's, I started handing out my résumé to everyone and anyone who would take it. I started with churches that were looking for pastoral staff. To be honest, I was expecting a flood of phone calls—after all, who wouldn't want to hire me? I had experience in a church of 50,000 people!

Silence.

Maybe they want to receive a few more résumés before getting back to me, I thought to myself. So to keep myself busy, I figured that I'd just work at Costco or Starbucks until the right opportunity rolled around—but they didn't call me back either. I even applied to teach English as a foreign language, which wasn't my favorite thing to do, but at least I had years of experience doing it.

Nothing. No one would call me back for an interview.

Perhaps God was trying to get my attention.

Doing Does Not Result in Done

Though I was devastated and ashamed to be back in Canada, I still fundamentally believed this lie—that as long as I found another job I was proud of doing, I'd be okay. After all, who wouldn't want to work with me?

Well, when no one called me back, I started wondering if the issue was less about the job market and more about me. So I stopped my search and began wrestling through some tough questions.

Why was I expecting a flood of phone calls? Why was I so confident that people wanted to work with me? Where was this sense of entitlement coming from? And why was I on such an emotional roller coaster?

When I would come across an open position that I could see myself doing, I'd be over the moon. But then, when I wouldn't hear anything back, I'd fall right back down into the pits of despair. I was constantly checking my email and making sure my ringer was on—it was quite obsessive—in case someone was trying to contact me for an interview. I was on this emotional roller coaster for months as I sent out what felt like hundreds of résumés.

Here's what I eventually realized about this lie: it never ends. There's no end to a life of doing. In fact, it's pretty much impossible to do enough. Even when you feel like you've accomplished all that you set your heart out to do, you will inevitably come across someone who has done more than you. So then what? Do you just do more by picking up another gig here, another side hustle there? And if so, for how long? Until you look like that miserable, scattered, anxious, dehydrated, and emotionless woman on the poster?

You are not what you do. Doing does not result in done. It only leads to more doing. In fact, there is no badge of honor in a life of doing—only exhaustion and despair.

What Happens When You Believe This Lie

If there's anyone who could speak to this, it would be King Solomon, the wisest and richest man of the ancient world. He had such a widespread reputation for wisdom and wealth that the infamous Queen of Sheba came to personally see it all for herself—and when she did, she couldn't believe her eyes. Upon observing "all of Solomon's wisdom, the palace he had built," the temple he constructed, and the way he lived, her breath was taken away. "She said to the king, 'The report I heard in my own country about your words and about your wisdom is true. But I didn't believe the reports until I came and saw with my own eyes. Indeed, I was not even told half. Your wisdom and prosperity far exceed the report I heard'" (1 Kings 10:4–7).

Solomon was the kind of guy who got whatever he wanted and whoever he wanted whenever he wanted. He was our culture's very definition of success, money, and power. However, when reflecting back on his life, he soon realized that it was all meaningless and futile, "'Absolute futility. . . . Everything is futile.' What does a person gain for all his efforts that he labors at under the sun?" (Eccles. 1:2–3). In fact, as it relates to the work he did and everything he accomplished, he went on to say, "I saw that all labor and all skillful work is due to one person's jealousy of another. This too is futile and a pursuit of the wind" (Eccles. 4:4).

Solomon made it to the top. He beat everyone out and he did all that he could do—by putting his nose to the grindstone and hustling. But when he looked up, he realized that it was all meaningless. He couldn't take anything with him. Eventually, his health would fail him, and he wouldn't even be able to enjoy all that he had amassed anymore. And when he died? Someone else would get it all. "And who knows whether he will be wise or a fool? Yet he will take over all my work that I labored at skillfully under the sun. This too is futile. So I began to give myself over to despair concerning all my work that I had labored at under the sun" (Eccles. 2:19–20).

So, if this is the end result of a life of doing—and of a life that believes the lie that you are what you do—is it worth it? If we can only partially and temporarily enjoy the benefits of all that we've done, is it worth living for? Is it worth building your life upon?

"You're in Control, So Make It Happen!"

The rise of the gig economy has made this ancient lie so compelling because it gives us the illusion of control. "You have unlimited earning potential," says the gig economy, "so if you want to go on a trip, just gig for a few hours. Want that new outfit? Sell a few things. Want the latest phone? Hustle for it. After all, everyone has free time that they waste, so just use that time and earn some extra cash. Be productive! You're in control, so make it happen—rise and grind and get it done."

It sounds harmless, doesn't it? After all, isn't gigging better than binging? Isn't working better than lounging?

In some respects you're right; it is far more productive. There's just one little issue—you're not actually in control.

This lie is so attractive because it makes us believe that we're God. That we have no limits. That we're in the driver seat of our lives and the masters of our own destiny—but we aren't. Earthquakes, hurricanes, stock market crashes, mass shootings, freak accidents, cancer, airplane delays, heavy snow storms, hackers, terrorists, sketchy Wi-Fi. Need I say more?

No matter how much of a planner you are, it's literally impossible to prepare for every single scenario, possibility, or permutation of life. You're not in control and you're not God, which means you can't actually do everything you want to do. If your self-definition comes from what you do, you're walking on thin ice. So you have two options: you can either ignore the reality of your limits and try to convince yourself you really can do anything you want, and therefore you really *are* what you do . . . or you can just stop believing the lie.

Conclusion

One day, when Jesus was teaching his followers on a mountainside, he mentioned a man by the name of Solomon—yes, the same Solomon that we've been talking about. He didn't talk about Solomon's wisdom or riches. He didn't bring up his lineage, nor did he mention anything the guy accomplished in his life—and there was *a lot* he could've talked about. In fact, rather than praising Solomon and urging his followers to imitate him, he did the opposite—he slammed him.

He compared all that Solomon amassed, built, and developed, with birds and flowers. That's right—with birds and flowers.

> "Consider the birds of the sky: They don't sow or reap or gather into barns, yet your heavenly Father feeds them. Aren't you worth more than they? Can any of you add one moment to his life span by worrying? And why do you worry about clothes?

Observe how the wildflowers of the field grow: They don't labor or spin thread. Yet I tell you that not even Solomon in all his splendor was adorned like one of these. If that's how God clothes the grass of the field, which is here today and thrown into the furnace tomorrow, won't he do much more for you—you of little faith?" (Matt. 6:26–30)

Friends, a life of doing only leads to a life of worrying. And as we've seen in this chapter and in Jesus' words, a life of worrying doesn't result in satisfaction—it just leads to more doing because there's no end to a life of doing. You're ultimately not in control—only God is. And no amount of doing can change that.

Chapter 2

Experiences > Things

A s a child, I enjoyed reading *certain* books.

Sure, I read when I had to write a book report for school, and also during those summer reading contests at the library. But other than that, reading didn't interest me much.

Perhaps it's because I grew up in the golden age of video games. Or maybe it was because *Seinfeld*, Hulk Hogan, and *The Fresh Prince of Bel-Air* were on TV. In any case, reading was never my first choice, so when I had to do it, I was quite selective.

I found myself going back to the same books over and over again. To be specific, it was *The Neverending Story* by Michael Ende, *Hatchet* by Gary Paulsen, and Todd Strasser's *Help! I'm Trapped in the First Day of School*. Now, I recognize that one of these is not like the others—the first one was made into a Hollywood film, the second one was awarded the Newberry Medal, and the last book can't even be found in libraries anymore—but for some reason, decades later, these are the three that have stuck with me.

Have you ever relived an experience from your past? When something or someone triggered a flashback, and it felt like you had jumped back in time? That's exactly how I felt when I came across this particular Coke commercial about the first day of college. Except my flashback wasn't about my first day of college. It was about being trapped in the first day of school—or to be more precise, how I *felt* when I read Strasser's book about it.

Here's the commercial.[1] A few somber chords are strummed on an electric guitar—it reminds me of the opening solo that Jeff Buckley plays on his rendition of the song "Hallelujah." It's the first day of college and outside in the courtyard freshmen are sitting alone, on their phones, sipping coffee, and waiting for class to start.

As these words make their way onto the screen, "First day of college, a day when talks and interactions are reduced to zero, so we thought of something special to make freshmen bond," the tempo suddenly picks up and the song transitions from a minor to major key.

And then, there appears—in the middle of the courtyard—an upright cooler, like the ones you see in gas stations. Except the Coke bottles inside of this one are free, since there's no lock, slot for coins, or buttons like on a vending machine. According to the caption on the screen, this is apparently "an excuse to break the ice and make them start talking."

As one backpack-strapped freshman after another sheepishly opens the cooler and grabs a bottle, they quickly notice that something's different. The cap can't be opened— at least, not in the traditional way.

The screen then pans to a guy and a girl standing beside each another. They clearly don't know each other and are both frustrated that their caps won't open. The caps look like those child safety lids that only open when you press down and twist. The problem is, these caps don't even work like that either.

After what seems like a while, they turn to one another and begin talking through the solution. And then, it happens! Their bottle caps meet. So with a smirk on their faces—at least the one on the guy's face is noticeable—they put their caps together and give it a friendly twist until, *pop!*

This happens over and over again throughout the rest of the commercial. Instead of freshmen sitting alone, now they're talking, connecting, laughing, and taking selfies with each other—all with nice and refreshing bottles of Coke.

What a brilliant commercial.

So basically, the moral of the story is that if I drink Coke, I'll never be awkward again, right? Coke will give me the confidence to approach strangers? To ask for that raise? To talk to that girl? To start that business? To come out of my introverted shell?

Flashbulbs, Being Awkward, and More Stuff

I hate awkward moments. Maybe that's why that book about reliving the first day of school has stuck with me over the years. As a freshman, everything's new, especially if you've moved. So when you add a new school onto new relationships and new routines—in addition to the inevitable sizing up that we tend to do to one another and the eventual social ranking that happens—it's just awkward.

And that's precisely why I love this Coke commercial. They've turned a perennially awkward experience on its head. They've reframed it by giving these freshmen an *experience* that they'll never forget.

Psychologists have a name for these sorts of unforgettable experiences. They call them flashbulb memories. We all have them. They can be public flashbulb memories like 9/11, JFK's assassination, the Columbine shooting, the raid on Osama bin Laden, or the Tiananmen Square massacre. They can also be personal ones, like your first kiss, the birth of a child, or a tragic death in the family.

Just think about where you were when you heard about 9/11. What were you doing? Who did you talk to? If you were alive when it happened, this experience is likely seared into your memory. And that's precisely how flashbulb memories work. They "are so emotionally important to us that they're laid down as vividly, completely and accurately as a photograph."[2]

I wonder if this is partially why experiences matter, and why we value them so highly. After all, don't they last longer than things?

Experiences Instead of Things

If I gave you $300, and you couldn't save it, use it to pay down debt, or give it away, what would you spend it on? Dinner and a movie? A night away? A quick trip to see friends or family? Or, would you get a new pair of jeans, sunglasses, or a small kitchen appliance?

In other words, would you spend your money on an experience or a thing?

Just check your credit card statement for a clue. It's fascinating how much you can learn about a person just by looking at a list of their recent transactions—and actually, how much data financial institutions have on us when it comes to our spending patterns. According to new research, it looks like we're now spending more money on experiences than things.[3]

In fact, when you break it down generationally, millennials are outspending Gen Xers and baby boomers on experiences. But don't get the wrong picture. Gen Xers and baby boomers aren't just working to pay off their mortgages and car payments, while millennials are jet-setting and airbnbing around everywhere. Each generation is spending money on experiences, it's just that millennials are spending a bit more.[4]

I love the way Joe Pine and James H. Gilmore describe this trend and how it's progressed over the years. They use the example of a birthday cake.[5]

Once upon a time, when we all lived on farms, if someone had a birthday, you'd eat a cake that was made from scratch with locally sourced, farm-fresh ingredients. It sounds hipster, but that was actually the only way you could get cake. You had to harvest your own grain and grind it into flour. Raise your own chickens to get eggs. Milk your own cows to get milk and make butter. And grow your own sugarcane for the sugar. In other words, you had to work with your hands and the *commodities* to get a cake.

Eventually, Betty Crocker came around. Her cakes tasted better, were more consistent, and she had access to more ingredients. Let's face it—buying her cake mix for your next birthday was a lot faster and simpler than farming all of the ingredients on your own. Sure, it was more expensive, but paying for this *good* (the cake mix) was easier than working with commodities.

Grocery stores eventually tuned in and figured out how profitable it would be to bake birthday cakes and sell them as a *service*. Of course, anyone could now buy the ingredients themselves without having to farm them. And sure, you could also buy the premade Betty Crocker cake mixes as well. But why do that when you could buy a birthday cake premade, pre-iced, and prepackaged?

This leads us to the present day. When my children were young, for their birthday parties, we sometimes bought premade cakes, and other-times my wife, Christina, made them herself. But generally, we hosted our children's parties at our house, at the park, and a few times at our church.

Not anymore. As our children are getting older, and life is getting busier, we've now resulted to outsourcing the party. Our girls had a joint party at a local jumpy house franchise that took care of everything—even writing the names down of who gave what for a present! The funny thing about these *experiences* was just how secondary the "thing"—I'm referring to the birthday cake—became.

Experiences Matter

Did you notice the progression? According to Pine and Gilmore, we've moved from commodities, to goods, to services, and now to experiences.[6] Experiences have become the new currency. In other words, amassing stuff and getting things aren't as valuable as experiences anymore. And even when we buy those new things, we're often buying them for the experiences that they will help create.

Have you ever unboxed an iPhone? Everything about it is an experience. The feeling of the box sliding open, the way that the phone is positioned, and how everything else is hidden underneath a little flap—it just flows. This is because Apple doesn't just create things; they create experiences.

Or how about golf? If you've ever been to Topgolf, you'll know just how much it puts the typical driving range to shame. Instead of lugging your clubs from your car, putting tokens into the ball machine, and finding a couple open spots so that you can hit together with your friends, everything is done for you at Topgolf. You reserve a bay that has sofas, tables, TVs, clubs, unlimited balls, and a computer that keeps score and suggests different games to play with your friends. There's even food and drink service! At Topgolf, you're not buying a bucket of balls; you're buying an experience.

Even buying a mattress has become an experience where people will Instagram themselves unboxing it! Casper has so revolutionized the mattress-buying experience that they've created a place called the Dreamery in New York City, where you can nap on their mattresses for forty-five minutes. Don't think about it like an open showroom with fluorescent lights. Instead, imagine a private pod with curtains, where you also get comfy pj's and drinks! It seems like there's no end to the possibilities experiences offer.

Lie #2: You Are What You Experience

If someone offered you an all-expenses-paid trip to anywhere in the world, would you take them up on it? You could go to Machu Picchu, the Great Barrier Reef, Everest, Santorini, or Phuket. You could even visit the Shire and Hobbiton in New Zealand where *The Lord of the Rings* was filmed.

Where would you go? What would you do?

There's just one catch. You have to go by yourself, and you can't bring your phone, camera, or tell anyone about it—ever. Would you still do it? Are you still excited? Or do you feel cheated?

Though I wish I could say that I'd be just as happy to go under these conditions, I don't know if I'd be up for it. The money-saving side of me says go, since it'd be a free trip, but every other fiber of my being tells me that I wouldn't end up enjoying it. Honestly, I think I'd rather save up and pay for the trip myself—so that I can go with my wife, take pictures, and share the experience with others—than go under these conditions. To never be able to share this experience with others would feel like torture to me.

Why is this? Do I care about getting a perfect Instagram picture *that* much? Is it because I want to humblebrag to my friends and family? "I'm having such a *hard time* figuring out how to pack for my free vacation to paradise. I can't believe I have to buy more luggage for this trip. What a drag."

Alright, maybe I'm overexaggerating, but what about after the trip? I don't want to hide everything that I experienced because it'd be a part of me. The experiences would be as real as the computer that I'm typing on. And as personal as the birthmark on my left hand. To not be able to share this once-in-a-lifetime travel experience would feel like I was hiding a part of myself from others. I'd feel dishonest, deceitful, and secretive.

It's All Around Us

Why is it so easy to identify with our experiences? Why do we believe this second lie that we are what we experience?

Because it's all around us. Remember the leeches from the Introduction? This lie—along with every other one in this book—is like a leech that has latched onto us.

It wasn't always like this though. While you might've lugged around a heavy film camera when you traveled on vacation, you probably didn't bring it around everywhere you went. And even when you got those shots, and eventually got the film developed and printed, you could only brag about it when people came over and looked through your photo albums. Not so today. For the average person, the camera on their smartphone has more features and power—and is a lot easier to use—than many interchangeable lens cameras. And the added benefit is that once you take the shot, you can share it immediately with your friends and family. It's just so convenient.

Now if the camera on your smartphone was just a matter of convenience, I wouldn't be bringing it up in this chapter. It's the fact that it functions like a gateway drug to a world of experiences that changes things quite a bit.

Yesterday, I was listening to "One Sweet Day," a classic duet from Boyz II Men and Mariah Carey. (I know the song is from 1995, but it's amazing.) When I heard my wife, Christina, coming downstairs, I called out to her from my office, turned up the music, and invited her to dance.

Lest you think I'm some romantic, keep reading.

I don't know what it is, but anytime I hug, kiss, or dance with Christina, our children always seem to appear out of nowhere and attempt to join in. This time, it was our son. He came into the office and started dancing beside us. Initially, it looked like he was dancing to some punk rock song, so when I told him to slow it down, he closed his eyes, started bending his knees, and began moving with the rhythm of the beat. It was adorable.

I wish I could've told you that I just smiled and continued to dance, but I didn't. I grabbed my smartphone and hit record. I don't know why, but I felt compelled to share this private experience publicly with others. Unfortunately and unintentionally, I exchanged a potentially romantic moment with my wife, and special memory with my family, for hundreds of views and likes on Instagram and Facebook.

This wouldn't have even been possible before smartphones. The experience used to be the reward, but now it doesn't seem to be enough. And since pictures of things don't get as much action on social media as pictures of experiences, we've started to see the world through the lens of potential likes and impressions.

It's a cycle. Go on an experience, snap a picture of it, and then share it online. And these days, don't forget to edit and put a filter on it first, or you'll run the risk of blending in, which will essentially cannibalize the number of likes you'll get! The more likes and followers you get from that picture, the more you want to go on another experience, so that you can get even more likes and followers.

And on and on it goes.

Heck, it's not even enough to go on vacation anymore— now you have to fill it with unique Instagrammable experiences. According to one study, more than 40 percent of millennials are now deciding where to vacation based on how Instagrammable it'll be (how well the pictures that they take will do on Instagram).[7] Likes have become a part of the experience.

I'm serious. It's a thing. No wonder it's so easy to believe the lie that we are what we experience.

You Are What You Experience

When the popular Instagram influencer, Essena O'Neill, decided to shut her account down, everyone thought she was crazy. She had more than half a million followers and was making $2,000 a post as an eighteen-year-old! According to our culture's definition of success, she had made it.

She was a part of this new industry called influencer marketing, which according to one estimate is now worth more than $1 billion.[8] On the one hand, it's not *that* different than a traditional celebrity endorsement, since the influencer is still getting paid—obviously less than a celebrity because they have fewer followers. On the other hand though—and maybe this is why it works and is a growing industry—the "sponsored ad" feels more authentic and organic. Perhaps this is why one study revealed that 70 percent of teenage YouTube subscribers trust influencer opinions over traditional celebrities.[9] And also why another study discovered that 86 percent of women turn to social media before making a purchase.[10]

The thing about influencer marketing is that it thrives on things and experiences—in fact, that's what it's about most of the time. Want to go to a posh five-star hotel for free? If you have enough engaged followers on Instagram, you can. Want to get paid to eat dinner? Do a sponsored post and you'll get more than just free food. Want a stroller, clothes, or a trip to Disney and more? Just have enough followers that trust you, and you'll find plenty of companies willing to spend their money to reach your audience.

Now can you see why there was so much noise when Essena shut it all down? By all standards, she was living "the dream." However, after realizing what a life pursuing "the dream" got her, she decided it wasn't worth it. After deleting more than two thousand pictures, which was her livelihood, she publicly wrote, "Online it looked like I had the perfect life . . . yet I was so completely lonely and miserable inside . . . I was lost, with serious problems so beautifully hidden . . . If anything, my social media addiction, perfectionist personality, and low self-esteem made my career. Oversexualization, perfect food photos, perfect travel vlogs—it is textbook how I got famous."[11]

I'm not saying that all influencer marketers are like this—in fact, many are simply trying to make a living— but if this is what eventually happened to one of the best, how can anyone say that they're immune? That it couldn't happen to them?

"May the Odds Be Ever in Your Favor!"[12]

Recognize the quote? It's from *The Hunger Games*—both the award-winning book and movie. After watching the first movie, I bought the trilogy of books and devoured them over Christmas vacation. I typically stick to non-fiction, but for some reason, I couldn't put these books down.

It wasn't because of the intriguing anti-institutional tones in the book, or because it so paralleled the struggle that our economy was going through after the 2008 recession. Rather, I found myself absorbed in *The Hunger Games* because it was a classic Cinderella story.

When Katniss Everdeen volunteers herself to be the tribute—aka the annual sacrifice—in place of her sister, Prim, there's a collective gasp, because to their district, "the word *tribute* is pretty much synonymous with the word *corpse*."[13] In the past seventy-four years, only two victors had ever emerged from their district. So if the past is the best predictor for the future, this means that Katniss only has a 3 percent chance of winning—not very favorable odds when the alternative is death. If you haven't read the book or watched the movie, here's some background about the Games that'll help you understand what I'm talking about.

> The rules of the Hunger Games are simple. In punishment for the uprising, each of the twelve districts must provide one girl and one boy, called tributes, to participate. The twenty-four tributes will be imprisoned in a vast outdoor arena that could hold anything from a burning desert to a frozen wasteland. Over a period of several weeks, the competitors must fight to the death. The last tribute standing wins. . . . To make it humiliating as well as torturous, the Capitol requires us to treat the Hunger Games as a festivity, a sporting event pitting every district against the others. The last tribute alive receives a life of ease back home, and their district will be showered with prizes, largely consisting of food. All year, the Capitol will show the winning district gifts of grain and oil and even delicacies like sugar while the rest of us battle starvation. "It is both a time for repentance and a time for thanks," intones the mayor.[14]

Can you see why the phrase "May the odds be ever in your favor" is so ironic? Especially when spoken to Katniss and her district, which never wins? It's not fair. It's not fair that kids have to fight to their death while the Capitol watches the Games as entertainment like a reality TV show. And it's not fair that though the Capitol is rich in resources, they only share resources with the winning district each year. It's just not fair. And here's the thing, this lie isn't fair either.

The Problem with This Lie

This lie that we are what we experience isn't fair because the odds are stacked against us. While it's great that social media gives us the opportunity to stay connected with our friends and family, our perception of reality gets distorted the longer we spend on it. For example, when's the last time you were scrolling through social media and noticed your best friend on vacation at the beach, a picture of a delicious meal from a coworker on a business trip, and your friend's new kitchen remodel, while you're sitting on your sunken-in couch, eating leftovers, and watching reruns of *Fixer Upper*?

It's impossible not to compare! Sure, you can like their photos and try to be happy for them, but when you *only* see their Instagram-worthy photos and not *everything else* that's going on behind the scenes for them—like the credit card debt used to finance that vacation and new kitchen, or the fact that your coworker is eating by himself at a restaurant while his family is thousands of miles away at home—it's impossible not to fall into the trap of comparison.

Our perception of *their* reality is distorted, since we only see the good times they're experiencing. After all, who takes a photo of their past-due bills? Of their children fighting? Of their stained carpet and scratched-up coffee table? Or, even better, of their picturesque laminate countertop, without a backsplash? No, God forbid that we post such things! It'd be too *real* and *authentic*.

This is how our perception of reality gets distorted, and why it's so easy to believe this lie. We're living in a constant state of comparison—not out of conscious choice, it's just a part of the air we're breathing. And what happens after you finally go on vacation and post a picture of that airplane wing, or that picturesque sunset? Are you satisfied? Or do you just want more?

Unfortunately, comparison only begets more comparison. Someone will always one-up you. Even if you had a better experience than others, how would you feel if they got more likes on social media? Or went on more experiences than you? And that's only half of it, since it's how *you* feel about them! How do you think *they* feel about you and your experiences?

Comparison is a zero-sum game. And underneath it all, there is no end to this lie. There is always more comparison. Instead of quenching the flames of jealousy and envy in our hearts, experiences end up fanning them. Because once the experience is over, it's over. Sure, you can buy a souvenir or make a scrapbook to commemorate that experience, but that'll only last so long until you want another experience, another high.

We saw this in the previous chapter with King Solomon who wrote that jealousy is the very thing that drives our grinding, hustling, striving, and working.[15] And after building his life on this shaky foundation and getting to the top—having experienced everything that there is to experience—he responded with these words.

> All things are wearisome, more than any-
> one can say. The eye is not satisfied by
> seeing or the ear filled with hearing. What
> has been is what will be, and what has been
> done is what will be done; there is nothing
> new under the sun. Can one say about any-
> thing, "Look, this is new"? It has already
> existed in the ages before us. There is no
> remembrance of those who came before;
> and of those who will come after there will
> also be no remembrance by those who fol-
> low them. (Eccles. 1:8–11)

Experiences are temporary, and a life driven to get more, do more, and have more experiences will only lead you further down a path that you might already be familiar with—a life filled with jealousy and envy.

Conclusion

In Essena's last YouTube video, she opened her heart and explained why she was leaving it all.

> I quit social media for my twelve-year-old self. When I was twelve, I told myself that I meant nothing and that I was worthy of nothing because I wasn't popular in life, a model, or beautiful by society's standards. At twelve, I obsessively stalked everyone who was that online. I looked up girls that were models, who were beautiful, and who were famous on YouTube. They had all of these likes, all of these views, and followers. And I thought . . . they would be so happy surrounded by all these people that loved them and appreciated them. I want that. I want to be valued . . . I told myself that when I had heaps of views, . . . I would feel valued, I would feel happiness . . . I let myself be defined by numbers and the

only thing that made me feel better about myself was more followers, likes, praise, and views . . . It was never enough . . . I was miserable. I had it all and I was miserable. Because when you let yourself be defined by numbers, you let yourself be defined by something that is not pure, that is not real, and that is not love.[16]

She realized in six years what it took Solomon a lifetime to figure out—that a life built on pursuing experiences does not satisfy.

Chapter 3

Me, Myself, and Maybe You

N etflix and chill.

Remember when that phrase *actually* used to mean curling up on the couch and binge-watching Netflix? Not so anymore. In our dating app-saturated hookup culture, those innocent days are long gone.

If you remember the early days of Match.com, eHarmony, and Christian Cafe, you *might've* created a profile, but you were definitely the exception if you met someone on any of those sites. And if you did end up meeting someone you were interested in, it was usually in view of a longer-term relationship, not a one-night stand.

Fast-forward to the rise of smartphones and apps like Tinder, Bumble, OkCupid, and Coffee Meets Bagel. While attitudes toward online dating are growing more positive, and all age groups under sixty-five are increasing in their usage of dating websites and apps, research shows that the majority of marriages of five years or less were initiated the old-fashioned way.[1]

So if online dating isn't an effective way to find your future spouse, what is it good for? And what are people using it for?

A sobering *Vanity Fair* article provides a glimpse into the rise of the hookup culture that's been attributed to dating apps like Tinder. Here's an excerpt:

> It's a balmy night in Manhattan's financial district, and at a sports bar called Stout, everyone is Tindering. The tables are filled with young women and men who've been chasing money and deals on Wall Street all day, and now they're out looking for hookups.
>
> "Guys view everything as a competition," he elaborates with his deep, reassuring voice. "Who's slept with the best, hottest girls?" With these dating apps, he says, "you're always sort of prowling. You could talk to two or three girls at a bar and pick the best one, or you can swipe a couple hundred people a day—the sample size is so much larger. It's setting up two or three Tinder dates a week and, chances are,

sleeping with all of them, so you could rack up a hundred girls you've slept with in a year." He says that he himself has slept with five different women he met on Tinder—"Tinderellas," the guys call them—in the last eight days.

In February, one study reported there were nearly one million people—perhaps fifty million on Tinder alone—using their phones as a sort of all-day, every-day, hand-held singles club, where they might find a sex partner as easily as they'd find a cheap flight to Florida. "It's like ordering Seamless," says Dan, the investment banker, referring to the online food-delivery service. "But you're ordering a person."[2]

The thing about these dating apps is that you can essentially be who you want to be—whenever, wherever, and to whomever. You can overemphasize the good, while hiding the not-so-pretty.

If you've both "swiped" right, you're a match; the next step is messaging. There's an art to texting and messaging over a dating app that's quite different than face-to-face, real-time conversations. For example, you can't message back too quickly; otherwise, you'll look desperate and *too* interested—even if you actually really like them. Sending question marks to see if they've received the message is also a faux pas for the same reasons. And if your text message takes up the whole screen—delete, delete, delete!

Can you see the way these dating apps have changed the way we relate to one another? Instead of being yourself and *mostly* saying what's on your mind, it's turned into a big cat-and-mouse game where everything is now heavily filtered. Essentially, social media has allowed us to edit ourselves in ways that were never before possible in real life.

Lie #3: You Are Who You Know

"I'm a . . . banana."

Wow, that was hard to get off my chest. Though I can admit it now, it's something I used to hide desperately.

It all started the year I moved from the sixth to seventh grade. Not only did I graduate from elementary school, but I went to a different high school than all of my friends. If that wasn't hard enough, the high school I went to had more Asians than non-Asians, which was a stark contrast to my nearly all-white elementary school. And though it might seem like this would be a welcome change, since I went from looking like the minority to the majority, I actually *felt* like I was moving from the majority to the minority.

On the outside I was yellow, but on the inside I was white—like a banana. I looked like a Korean, ate like a

Korean, understood Korean when my parents spoke to me, and also went to a Korean church, but that was about it. On the inside, I was Canadian—I spoke like a Canadian, thought like a Canadian, and acted like one too.

So in elementary school, as a proud Canadian, my favorite thing to do was to play hockey—before school, during recess, at lunch, after school, and on the weekends when I wasn't watching Hockey Night in Canada. Unfortunately, after stepping foot into a high school full of students ranging from seventh to twelfth grade, I had to retire my hockey stick. On the asphalt rink, I just wasn't strong enough, tall enough, or fast enough to play with the big kids.

What a wretched first year of high school that was. At my new school, not only was I mourning the loss of hockey, but I didn't know who was popular, so I just made friends with whoever paid attention to me. And for that one person who did, I eventually came to realize that he was the loser-loner that everyone made fun of. Although we got along really well, by the end of seventh grade, I started to wonder why we had become friends when he had gone to elementary school with nearly everyone else in the grade. Why didn't he ever hang out with anyone else? Did he not have any friends? And were people talking behind our backs?

When I realized what was going on, as a *confident* thirteen-year-old who *didn't care* what anyone else thought, I did the natural thing that everyone else had already done years ago—I ditched him. I ditched my only friend, in hopes that it would elevate my social cachet and lead to a seat with the cool kids in the cafeteria—how shameful.

I believed the lie that my worth and value came from who I knew. So once I realized that the most popular kids were the immigrants from Korea—who I conveniently looked like—I figured that the quickest path to popularity was to dress like them and talk like them, so that I could hang out with them.

The only issue was that I didn't know how to speak Korean—other than a few words here and there. And I definitely didn't dress like the cool Korean kids either. So after burning my Wrangler jeans from Walmart, I rented Korean drama VHS tapes and K-Pop music videos from the Korean grocery store so that I would know how to act and dress. I spent way too much time in online chat rooms with Koreans in Korea, so that I would learn how to talk like them. I even went to the extreme of telling my parents that I wouldn't speak to them again in English, since I wanted full immersion.

It was driving everything for me—this lie that my identity came from the people I associated with, that I am who I know.

The problem was, no matter how much I edited myself by speaking like a Korean and dressing like a Korean, I was never fully accepted by the Koreans at school. Sure, they invited me to their parties and let me hang around with them, but since I was a banana, there seemed to be an invisible wall between us. At times I felt accepted, but when I'd turn around, they'd be shaming me. It was a constant cycle of acceptance and rejection. In their words, I would never fit in because I was a banana; and there was nothing I could do to change it.

Why Is CrossFit So Popular?

In recent years, working out *together* seems to be on the rise. But do you remember when that wasn't the case? When working out in your home was all the rage? If you dig deep into your past (or just look for the meme), you might remember those late-night Total Gym infomercials featuring Chuck Norris and Christie Brinkley. If not, try to remember why you (or your parents) bought that Bowflex, ThighMaster, or Ab Roller that you can't even get rid of at a garage sale anymore.

In the last several years, why do you think Barre, Orangetheory Fitness, and CrossFit have exploded? And why do their followers seem so obsessive about their gyms and their workouts—both online and in real life? While each of them have their own method designed to get you fit, it's the community that seems to be the sticking point and why people can't stop talking about it—especially those CrossFitters.

If you don't believe me, here's an experiment. Post this question on social media and watch the responses roll in: "If you #CrossFit, why? What are the things you love about it? And hate about it?" Here are a few of the responses I received:

> "The community is a huge part of it. The last person to complete the WOD (workout of the day) gets celebrated the loudest."
> —Stafford Greer

> "CrossFit is so great because of the community. Does it help you get strong and fit? Yes. Is it scalable to every age and ability? Yes. Is it the closest thing to a team dynamic from your old sports team? Yes. But the big draw is community. Believing in each other, helping each other, rooting for the very last person to finish. It is a place to belong and to connect. And get ripped." —Nathan McWherter

> "The community was amazing. Monthly socials, celebrating birthdays, phone calls to check up on each other, and traveling

with friends to have weekend getaways. We also had phenomenal support from our CrossFit community after a major event in our life . . . it really can be a solid community." —Patty Rooker

The interesting thing about CrossFit is that you can do it anywhere. You don't necessarily need to pay the pricy gym membership fee to learn the techniques. In fact, the workout of the day is posted for free online, in addition to thousands of free videos on YouTube. So how did CrossFit get to be a $4-billion brand?[3] How is it possible that there are more CrossFit gyms around the world than there are Starbucks locations in the United States? And having only been founded in the year 2000, how is it that they have their own Games like the Olympics?

It's because the founders of CrossFit understand the power of community and its uncanny ability to create magnetic connections between humans. They understand that those around you often hold the greatest power to shape you.

Isn't that precisely why who you know—both in real life and online—matters more than ever before? Just consider the influence that others have on where you work, what happens at work, how you feel after work, your love life (or absence thereof), and your emotional, physical, and spiritual health. No wonder it's so easy to believe this lie that you are who you know.

"Alexa, Enable Away Mode"

Did you know that this command will trigger Alexa to play a series of conversations and noises to trick a potential thief into thinking that the house is full? While interacting with digital personal assistants like Siri, Alexa, and Google Assistant has become increasingly normal, they all have the same purpose—to make your life more convenient. After all, when's the last time you asked one of them what the weather was outside, or to text someone back?

Actually, let me backtrack, they all *used* to have the same purpose.

In the last few years, Gatebox, the Japanese start-up, and the Korean tech giant, SK Telecom, have both created two-dimensional personal assistants that you can see, interact with, and emotionally develop a relationship to. You can text Hikari, Gatebox's assistant, and she'll text back. When she sees you come home, she'll smile. And if there's a special occasion you want to celebrate, she can even share a toast with you.[4] Wendy, who is SK Telecom's digital assistant, is even able to listen, understand, and react to you using her words and facial expressions! While both of them live inside of a cylindrical fish-tank like device, Wendy can even jump into your smartphone to accompany you for a night out on the town.[5]

How has this become a thing? Have we somehow run out of interesting people on Earth so that we now have to use robots and artificial intelligence for companionship?

At least Hikari and Wendy are two-dimensional and PG. The pornography industry has already come out with three-dimensional robots—male and female—that you can have sex with. What's next? Sex robots that you can program to look like, talk like, and act like *real* people you know? Futurist Mark Penn, in his book *Microtrends Squared*, believes it's only a matter of time.[6]

Perhaps this is taking things farther than you're comfortable with, but it's an indication of the shifts that are taking place in our culture when it comes to relationships, love, and sex. So, if the people around you aren't shaping you, I guess you can always resort to Siri, Alexa, Hikari, or Wendy.

~~You Are Who You Know~~

"Early in life, did you ever have a fear of abandonment?"

"Oh yeah, it's a primal fear for any child . . . it dictates a lot of how you deal with life."[7]

If it were not for the HBO documentary *Robin Williams: Come Inside My Mind*, Dave Itzkoff's biography *Robin*, and the countless number of articles written on him after his suicide, we wouldn't have known *that* side of Robin Williams.

Although I remember him best as the Genie from *Aladdin*, as Sean from *Good Will Hunting*, and as Mrs. Doubtfire, it's sobering to see the patterns of loneliness and isolation that plagued Williams throughout his life.

Everyone who knew Robin from his thirty-five years in show business knew him as one of America's most beloved and charismatic comedians, actors, and voices. Friends and family knew him as a hard worker, brave and bold, a loving father, and a considerate friend. But in the final months before his death, though his physical ailments and anxiety were on the rise, no one saw it coming. In fact, the night before his suicide, according to his wife, all signs indicated that he was getting better.[8]

You would think that being one of the most connected, networked, and recognizable celebrities in the world would lead to a sense of fulfillment, right? To know that others would drop everything to spend time with you should lead to a sense of acceptance, security, and love, no?

This lie that you are who you know is like fog. It's everywhere and elusive. You see it all around you, you can feel the coolness of it, and you see others enwrapped in it, but when you try to grab it, you can't—it just dissipates. And a life built on this lie doesn't lead to the thing it promises: greater levels of meaningful connection with others. Ironically, it actually produces the exact opposite: isolation.

Connection and Disconnection

We are now more connected as a society than ever before. When traveling to speak, I use FaceTime to be a part of my children's bedtime routine. Viber is the instant messaging app I use to stay in touch with my parents and siblings. And Facebook, Instagram, and Twitter are my apps of choice to stay connected with friends and acquaintances.

Isn't this night and day from what it used to be? Remember when you had to pay long-distance fees to call someone outside of your *city*? When Christina's parents were dating long distance, her dad would call her mom once a week on payday using a payphone and a roll of quarters! Now you can call anyone in the world for free using an app.

So if we're more connected than we've ever been, and it's easier (and cheaper) to stay in touch with others, why are we growing isolated? Is it because of the Internet, smartphones, and the rise of the gig economy?

Two decades ago when Robert Putnam wrote *Bowling Alone* to investigate why our society was growing increasingly disconnected, the Internet was booming—but it was in its infancy. Facebook didn't exist, and neither did Myspace.

In fact, other than a few instant messaging services, the Internet had no *social* aspect about it. Back then, it was all about finding information, rather than connecting with others. What a far cry from today!

As we've explored throughout this chapter, there's no doubt that the Internet has vastly accelerated our growing connection *and* disconnection from one another, but as Putnam argues, it definitely wasn't the cause of it.

> The timing of the Internet explosion means that it cannot possibly be casually linked to the crumbling of social connectedness. . . . Voting, giving, trusting, meeting, visiting, and so on had all begun to decline while Bill Gates was still in grade school. By the time that the Internet reached 10 percent of American adults in 1996, the nationwide decline in social connectedness and civic engagement had been under way for at least a quarter of a century. . . . The Internet may be part of the solution to our civic problem, or it may exacerbate it, but [it] was not the cause.[9]

In a similar way, while the ubiquity of smartphones and the rise of the gig economy are not the cause for our growing disconnectedness with one another, they may just be the very things that are rapidly accelerating it.

Just consider the implications surrounding our smartphone usage. The majority of all smartphone owners rarely or never turn their phones off. They always have it with them wherever they go.[10] In fact, according to one study from Deloitte, Americans are now checking their smartphones an average of fifty-two times per day! No wonder tech companies like Apple and Instagram have rolled out features to help individuals track and limit their personal usage.[11] And let's not forget what Vitaminwater recently did! They launched a contest to give $100,000 to one lucky individual who was willing to stay off their smartphone for a year.[12]

Why would they do this? And what do you think the obsessive usage of our smartphones is doing to us?

It's amazing how our smartphones have created this sense of constant connection with others. Just think about the way you said goodbye to a friend who was moving away twenty years ago versus in the past couple of years. Back then, you never knew if you were going to see or talk to them again. But now, goodbyes don't seem to be as dramatic since we are constantly connected to one another online.

So if we're constantly connected to one another due to our smartphones, how is it possible that our phones are simultaneously leading us to disconnection and isolation?

Well, have you ever used your phone in front of others? Choosing to scroll through social media, read the news, or answer emails, instead of engaging in a conversation with those around you? And what about the last time you were at a coffee shop or restaurant with another person? Was your phone face up, so that you didn't miss whatever it is that you were waiting for? That's how.

In fact, if you've ever done this, you're in good company because a third of those officially surveyed in 2014 admit to occasionally using their phones to avoid interacting with others in public spaces.[13] Six years later, in a few of my unofficial surveys, it's over 80 percent. Why are we opting out of present, embodied moments to scroll through other people's past experiences on a screen?

And while freedom is the allure of the gig economy— that you will have more flexibility in your schedule to spend time with your loved ones, and money to spend on experiences—it actually leads to the opposite. Just consider the free time or downtime that you used to have after work to invite friends over for dinner, to talk with your neighbors, or go to the lake with your family on the weekends. Haven't you replaced some or all of it with hustling, grinding, and working on the side, *so that* you'll have more money to spend time with them . . . at some point in the future?

Do you see the false logic in that? You're giving up free time to work, so that you'll have more money for free time in the future. How does this make sense? To exchange present moments of real connection for future moments of hopeful connection? What if that future moment never comes? Or what if the lack of time spent with them now, leads to them not even wanting to spend time with you in the future? And that's if they're even still around.

This lie is so deceptive. On the surface, while the Internet, smartphones, and the rise of the gig economy appear to be connecting us with one another, they're actually doing the very opposite. They're exacerbating the problems of disconnection, isolation, and loneliness. We are more disconnected than ever before, which is leading to a decline in trust. And the more disconnected and untrusting we become, the more we are going to turn inward and become unhealthily obsessed with ourselves.

The Connection Between Disconnection and Obsession

Are you familiar with the parable of the rich fool? I'd tell it myself, but Jesus does it better.

> "A rich man's land was very productive. He thought to himself, 'What should I do, since I don't have anywhere to store my crops? I will do this,' he said. 'I'll tear down my barns and build bigger ones and store all

my grain and my goods there. Then I'll say
to myself, "You have many goods stored up
for many years. Take it easy; eat, drink, and
enjoy yourself.'" (Luke 12:16–19)

What I love about Jesus' parables is that they're as appli-
cable today in the twenty-first century, as they were in the
first century. And what's amazing is that the more you dig,
the more you'll find—this is true for the entire Bible. For
example, while the crowds listening in on Jesus would've
been shocked by the story, it's likely for different reasons
than us. Here's why.

On the surface, it seems foolish that the man would first
tear down his barns before building bigger ones. Perhaps
his older barns were dilapidated? Or maybe he didn't have
enough land for additional barns? Both seem unlikely
because this man was *already* rich, even before his year of
plenty, which means he likely took care of his property. And
it's not like we're talking about Manhattan here, so the fact
that he already had more than one barn shows us that he
likely had room to build more. So why didn't he just add
on to his additional barns? And if he was already rich, why
didn't he give some of his crops away?

While these are the questions that naturally come to
mind for a twenty-first-century reader, Jesus' initial listeners would've been shocked for different reasons. Try reading
through the parable again and counting how many times

the rich man uses the personal pronoun. And did you notice to whom he was speaking to?

In Jesus' day, this is not how people functioned. Ancient Near Eastern culture was not individualistic; people didn't grow their own fiefdoms and keep their wealth to themselves. Rather, life was lived together, with one another, and in community.

So why is this rich man isolated and making the decision by himself? Especially when his decision would affect everyone else around him? How long has he been isolated and disconnected from those around him? How long has it been since he's trusted someone else? And how long has he lived inside of his own vacuum of reality?

No wonder he's become so obsessed with himself. Isolation is the end result of disconnection. I love how King Solomon puts it, "One who isolates himself pursues selfish desires; he rebels against all sound wisdom" (Prov. 18:1).

The more disconnected and isolated you become, the more you'll turn inward and grow obsessed with yourself. Eventually, my current needs, my future needs, and my contingent *what-if* needs, will be all that you can think of. Even when you're "helping" others, it will always be in view of what you can get out of it, or for that time when they can pay you back. And instead of recognizing and being grateful for the role that others have played in your life, you will reframe and reinterpret reality through the lens of me, myself, and I.

This is how it happens. After getting a promotion, you begin thinking to yourself, *I got this because I deserved it*, rather than recognizing the role your boss and teammates played. Or after receiving an admissions letter, you begin saying to yourself, *Wow, all those years of hard work paid off*, instead of being grateful for the sacrifices that your parents made, and the role that your teachers and mentors had in your education.

It's a vicious cycle.

The more you turn inward and reinterpret the past through this self-centered obsessive way, the more disconnected you'll become. And the more you disconnect from others, the more you'll see life through the lens of giving and taking. Your relationships with others will turn into meaningless consumeristic transactions. And instead of viewing life with an abundance mind-set, you'll begin seeing everything through the lens of scarcity. Instead of living a life of generosity, you'll scrape by with greed. And on and on it goes.

Conclusion

I wanted her to see me. I wanted her to want me. I wanted her to need me. And I was willing to be whoever I needed to be to make it happen.

Have you ever had thoughts like these? Where you were willing to edit yourself? Change whatever you needed to change? And essentially become whoever you needed to become just to fit in, be accepted, or feel loved?

I know I have.

Before marrying Christina, I was addicted to pornography. With one of my previous girlfriends, I was addicted to sex. And when I would meet a woman I was attracted to, those were the thoughts that drove everything for me.

The thing is, none of it was ever enough. No amount of masturbation, pornography, lust, or sex satisfied that longing I had to connect with others, to know another person intimately, to be known as I really am, and to feel accepted. The morning after, I was never content. Sure, for a fleeting moment I would feel a sense of connection, but shortly after, feelings of shame and guilt would arrive like the tide and wash away all remnants of what was. And every single time, without fail, I would always feel alone—even if there was someone beside me.

Other people do not satisfy. They cannot satisfy the longings that drive us to them. In fact, even a spouse can't ultimately satisfy that deeper longing we all have to know and be known. You are not who you know.

Chapter 4

The American Dream

What is the American Dream? And how do you know you've achieved it? Is it the result of a life filled with grit, grind, hustle, and determination? Is it about owning a single-family home on a quarter acre, being your own boss, and being able to grill out and eat apple pie whenever you want? Or is it actually more about securing equality and justice for all? Or perhaps, is the American Dream ultimately about living a life of flexibility, experiences, and a four-hour workweek?

And just so we're clear here, as a Korean-Canadian, I'm not just talking about the United States when referring to the American Dream. I'm referring to that intangible human desire that we all have for freedom, security, and "enough" money—whatever "enough" might mean to you. Other names for it are *la dolce vita* in Italian or *leven als God in Frankrijk* in Dutch.

So here's the real question: If there were a silver bullet to achieving the American Dream, what would it be?

As you might've already guessed if you're familiar with my other books, I don't believe in a silver bullet. In fact, when Forbes created the multitiered "American Dream Index" to attempt to measure progress toward it, they busted that myth. They based it on seven metrics: "bankruptcies, building permits, goods-producing jobs, labor participation rate, layoffs, start-up activity, and unemployment insurance claims."[1]

Though I'm grateful for their Index, it's ultimately not that useful because it's like a thermometer—it's read-only. Something would need to change for this Index to function like a thermostat, and only then could it actually contribute to moving toward that elusive Dream.

"Aren't Schools Factories?"

If you wanted to stir the pot, this is how you'd do it. Walk into a local school and ask the principal how many widgets they produced on their assembly line last year. Then specifically ask to see their P&L statement, their debt ratio, their EBITDA, and the size of their cash reserves. I'm sure you can anticipate the response—they'd be appalled that you were comparing them to a business or a factory. And though they would be right in their response, there are actually more similarities than the school's administration might realize.

While I'll summarize their arguments here, if you've never noticed a connection between our education system and the industrial revolution, you're not alone. Do yourself a favor and read Seth Godin's manifesto on education, *Stop Stealing Dreams*. Alternatively, you can also watch one of Ken Robinson's short TED Talks to get the gist.

Believe it or not, there was a time when children didn't have to go to school in America. Education wasn't mandatory and many children worked in factories. However, in 1918, when nationwide compulsory education was put in place, factory owners pushed back hard because they couldn't afford to hire adults. Here's how, according to Godin, they were ultimately convinced and how it has correspondingly affected the way our education system functions today:

> Part of the rationale used to sell this major transformation to industrialists was the idea that educated kids would actually become more compliant and productive workers. . . . The plan: trade short-term child-labor wages for longer-term productivity by giving kids a head start in doing what they're told. Large-scale education was not developed to motivate kids or to create scholars. It was invented to churn

out adults who worked well within the system. . . . Every year, we churn out millions of workers who are trained to do 1925-style labor. . . . The bargain (take kids out of work so we can teach them to become better factory workers as adults) has set us on a race to the bottom. . . . Here's the question every parent and taxpayer needs to wrestle with: Are we going to applaud, push, or even permit our schools (including most of the private ones) to continue the safe but ultimately doomed strategy of churning out predictable, testable, and mediocre factory workers? As long as we embrace (or even accept) standardized testing, fear of science, little attempt at teaching leadership, and most of all, the bureaucratic imperative to turn education into a factory itself, we're in big trouble.[2]

If it's true that much of our modern-day Western education system has been influenced by industrial age factory work, then it's safe to assume that the same values that used to permeate factories are also present in schools. Standardization, compliance, order, structure, control, discipline, and fear. Sound familiar? Just think back to your schooling days. Were you ever subjected to standardized tests, truancy cops, periods, drills, pop quizzes, homeroom, detention, or teaching tactics like shame, guilt, embarrassment, and humiliation to keep you in order?

An Empty Bag of Lies

Are millennials and subsequent generations being fed a bag of lies? Is student debt *actually* good debt? And just because it might've been true in the past, how do we know whether or not it still stands true today?

The promise was, "If you get to class, do your homework, participate in extracurricular activities, and score well on standardized tests, you'll get into a highly ranked college. And though you'll graduate with five or six figures of student debt, once you graduate from a top college, you'll have your pick of companies to work for. And with that well-paying job, it'll only take you a few years to pay off that debt, which will put you on track to achieving the American Dream! So student debt *is* good debt."

While this might have been true for everyone who graduated from college and entered the workforce before the 2008 recession—which includes older millennials and previous generations—it's a different story for younger millennials and the next wave of young workers, Gen Z.

After the recession hit, younger millennials fresh out of college and burdened with a ridiculous amount of student debt were competing against laid-off boomers, Gen Xers, and older millennials—who had a lot more experience and a much broader network—for the *same* jobs. If a younger millennial was lucky enough to land a job fresh out of college, it was likely an internship, rather than the full-time permanent position that they *would've* been hired for if they had only graduated pre-2008.

So is student debt *actually* good debt? And is going to a top college worth the higher tuition fees—especially for those who graduated post-2008? When studying previous recessions, Wendy Rahn, a political science professor at the University of Minnesota, discovered "that those who happened to be unlucky enough to have entered the labor market in a recession may never really recover from it." Part of this has to do with the fact that historically, during previous recessions, there were fewer opportunities and lower starting wages. And when those two factors are put together, students end up paying more interest because it'll take longer to pay off their student debt. But ultimately, this directly affects their lifetime earnings, which "tend to hinge on an individual's first decade in the workforce, with those who earn less as they begin their careers never catching up," according to the economists at the Federal Reserve.[3]

As the effects of the recession are wearing off, perhaps things will be different for the very youngest of millennials and Gen Zers. Perhaps it'll be easier for them to find a well-paying job and pay off their student debt. Or maybe they're just going to be worse off because tuition costs have doubled over the last twenty years for private universities and tripled for public universities.

How does it make sense that "the cost of college has risen almost three times as fast as wages?"[4] And who gets to determine whether or not a school is a top school anyway? Are you actually guaranteed a better paying job if you go to a higher ranked school? Do you really get an exponentially better level of education that directly corresponds with the higher tuition fees? And does your long-term happiness go up as your school's ranking goes up? Or—is going to a top school more about fame and the brand name?

Lie #4: You Are What You Know

When Thomas Jefferson wrote that knowledge was power and ignorance was weakness, he was onto something.[5] What's interesting is that more than a century later, the authoritarian dictators Hitler and Pol Pot would've said the same thing—they just would've applied it differently.

While Jefferson had as much in common with Hitler and Pol Pot as oil has with water, it's interesting to see how their differing beliefs on the power of knowledge played out in their leadership. For Jefferson, it was the creation of local state universities in Virginia. For Hitler it was the burning of tens of millions of "un-German" books on their quest to create *new* knowledge.[6] And for Pol Pot, it was the genocide of his *own* people, specifically the "intellectuals, professors, businesspeople, and college-educated citizens."[7]

All three deeply understood the power that knowledge has to shape and form our identities, they just wanted to do something different with it. Jefferson wanted to freely promote knowledge, while Hitler and Pol Pot wanted to control and restrict it. Generations later, we see the difference. While Hitler's actions are inexcusable, he didn't kill *all* the educated; in fact, he was more concerned about his ideal Aryan race than about education levels. Pol Pot, on the other hand, killed an entire generation of the educated in Cambodia—and its effects are still felt today.

The 1975 to 1978 genocide in Cambodia is partly why there's such a general disinterest in childhood education there. Just consider the fact that the majority of children in Cambodia's neighboring country, Thailand, have access to secondary and higher education institutions, compared to only 2 percent of Cambodian children. "As one Thai teacher working in Cambodia explained, 'In Thailand the children have dreams to go to university, and many of them do. In

Cambodia, the children are not allowed to dream like this. This dream is unheard of.'"[8]

Isn't this precisely why knowledge is power?

An Incurable Disease

Imagine trying to find a cure for a disease that was affecting 3.5 million people in twenty-one countries in Asia and Africa—and you couldn't use vaccines, medicine, or surgery. Oh yeah, and if you don't find a cure, this disease can lead to disability and amputations, or in some cases death. *No pressure.*

This is not a hypothetical situation—it's called Guinea worm disease, and if you have a weak stomach, you might want to skip to the next paragraph. But for the rest of you brave ones, here's the quick description of these satanic little things. The disease starts with unclean water. In some ponds, there are tiny freshwater crustaceans that have swallowed Guinea worm larvae. So when you drink the dirty pond water, you're also drinking these larvae that hatch into worms, which then grow inside of your body. At some point, these Guinea worms eventually escape out of your foot, hand, breast, or eye socket by exuding burning acid to create a blister on your skin. To find relief for this burning pain, you jump into the nearest pond, which unfortunately triggers the Guinea worm to then release millions of larvae into the pond, thus perpetuating the cycle . . . I told you they were satanic.[9]

Since 1987, fighting these things has been the life work of Dr. Donald Hopkins, who is now the special advisor for Guinea worm eradication, after serving as the director of all health programs at The Carter Center. What's miraculous is that, thirty years later, Guinea worm disease has been reduced by 99.99 percent! And in 2017, only thirty people were affected—yet there is still no vaccine, medicine, or cure.[10]

So how did he do it?

He leveraged the power of knowledge. He figured that since there was no medical cure, perhaps the cure was in educating the rural poor about it: how it gets contracted, how to prevent it from spreading, and how to treat it once you have it. For the Guinea worm, this can be translated into three steps:

1. Don't drink nonfiltered pond water.
2. If you get infected, don't jump into a public water supply, no matter how much it burns; get treated instead.
3. If a neighbor isn't filtering their water or if they become infected, you have to teach and help them.[11]

Turns out, some things really can be fixed with more knowledge. No wonder this lie that you are what you know is so widespread.

AP Classes, Extra Credit, and Summer School for "Fun"

There were no joy rides or last hurrahs in the summers before my junior and senior years of high school. Instead of going on vacation, traveling, or hanging out at the beach, I went to summer school for "fun." I wasn't there to repeat classes that I had failed during the school year. I actually went to pre-emptively get ahead and preview future classes, so that I'd get better grades during the school year.

That's what life was like for me growing up. At school, I took AP classes instead of the normal ones. For extra credit, I remember entering a titration chemistry competition at the local university. After school, in addition to homework and violin practice, I had to do Kumon math drills, and work with an English tutor who taught me that when I write "on the other hand" in a sentence, I need to first start with "on the one hand." And if that wasn't enough, I also went to Korean school and orchestra rehearsal on the weekends. Everything was about getting ahead, so that I could get unconditional early acceptance into a top-tier Canadian university.

My parents were so intense about memorization and knowledge being the key to getting ahead that I didn't even have any chores at home. In fact, one time I was scolded by my mom because I tried washing the dishes after dinner. She sent me to my room because, apparently, my time was better spent studying.

I'm not griping or complaining. After all, the reason I have such an insatiable love for learning is likely a result of the way my parents raised me. And for that, I'm grateful, because leaders are learners. In fact, if you were to survey the "movers and shakers" of society—especially since gigging and side hustling are rapidly becoming the new normal—you would quickly notice a pattern in their lives. Phrases like, "I don't know how to do that," or, "that's not what I went to school for," would never come out of their lips.

So if you have an eye for art, you can learn how to design logos or animate GIFs on Skillshare. With that new skill, you can then earn a little extra cash on the side bidding for jobs on Fiverr, Upwork, or 99designs. Alternatively, if you're a technophile but don't know how to code, you can learn how to make your own app by logging into Lynda.com and taking a course.

Since there's no shortage of learning opportunities, is knowledge *actually* enough? Sure, the best leaders are learners, but all learners aren't leaders. So does knowing more really result in getting ahead?

~~You Are What You Know~~

Dangerous Minds with Michelle Pfeiffer or *Dead Poets Society* with Robin Williams—which was your favorite movie? While they might seem completely different upon first glance, they're actually quite similar in many respects. Both feature unconventional teachers who, though initially met with much skepticism, end up earning the trust and love of their students. They both use poetry to get through to their students—Robin Williams does so by asking his students to rip out the introduction from their poetry textbook, while Michelle Pfeiffer uses the lyrics of a couple Bob Dylan songs. In both movies, a student dies. And in both, knowledge is presented as the key to a better life.

The setting is where the differences begin. *Dead Poets Society* takes place in an all-male elite conservative boarding school in Vermont, whereas *Dangerous Minds* takes place in a public high school in a low-income neighborhood. The class in *Dead Poets Society* is all white, compared to the multi-ethnic class in *Dangerous Minds*. And socioeconomically speaking, the characters in each movie couldn't be further apart from each other.

There's a reason both were successful at the box office. They fed into the deeply cherished lie that education is the silver bullet to achieving the American Dream. They painted a distorted picture of reality by minimizing the effect that your background and upbringing have on your future success in life. "Just study enough and you'll make it." "As long as you have one great teacher who believes in you, you will overcome all odds." "Everyone starts with an A, it's up to you whether or not you'll keep it."

I wonder if this is why J. D. Vance's memoir, *Hillbilly Elegy,* became a *New York Times* bestseller? Vance achieved the American Dream, after all. Even though he grew up in a rural dead-end town, he was able to escape and become successful because he worked hard enough at life and school. So, if it's possible for him, shouldn't it be possible for everyone?

Are these all just one-off stories—anomalies, myths, or fairy tales designed to give us false hope? Or does knowing more really result in getting ahead?

Schools Are Still Segregated

Though segregation has been outlawed for quite some time, it still exists in subtle ways. I'm not talking about restaurants, designated seating on public transportation, or separate restrooms based on your ethnicity. I'm referring to segregated schools—based on the socioeconomic status of your parents and where you live.

This isn't breaking news. In fact, it's been public knowledge since 1966 when James Coleman presented a 737-page research report to the president and Congress of the United States. According to Section 402 of the Civil Rights Act of 1964, Coleman was required to write a research report "concerning the lack of availability of equal educational opportunities for individuals by reason of race, color, religion, or national origin in public educational institutions."[12] The only problem was that the Office of Education wasn't pleased with the findings—so they tried to cover it up. They called it incendiary and decided to release it on July 2, 1966, which was the Saturday of the Fourth of July weekend.

In his report, Coleman examined how well children were learning and what influenced their capacity to learn, rather than merely gathering information on how governmental resources were being directed and used by schools. And though he discovered that racial segregation still existed— which made sense, since it had only been two years since the Civil Rights Act was passed—that's not why his research was covered up.

According to a report published fifty years later, Coleman's research got covered up because, backed with data, it unearthed something that no one had ever said before. The amount of funding that the school received and the physical amenities of the school were not the two greatest predictors of a student's success. Rather, it was the educational background of the student's family, and the diversity of their classroom.[13]

In other words, success is not a direct result of how prestigious of a school you go to. The family you were born into and the diversity of your classroom—things that you have no control over—might actually matter more to your success than anything else, even including your test scores. So is knowledge the great equalizer? Has it ever been? Will it ever be?

Trying to Reinvent the Broken Education System

Recently, *Time* magazine highlighted what it was like to be a teacher in America. Hope Brown is a fifty-two-year-old full-time history teacher in Kentucky. Although she has a master's degree and has been teaching for sixteen years, she needs to work a few side hustles just to make ends meet. So she sells her plasma, consigns her clothes, and runs a historical tour company with her husband.

Binh Thai is a forty-one-year-old humanities teacher in New York City. Although he has two masters' degrees, to afford the cost of living, he's had to work two or three jobs for the last fifteen years. And it's not like he's living alone either! He's splitting the rent with his roommate.

Misty McNelley is a thirty-one-year-old English teacher in Oklahoma. In addition to teaching full-time, she works part-time as a veterinary technician, and owns a photography business as a side hustle. Her husband also works, but they're still not sure whether they can afford to have another child.[14]

If Nelson Mandela was right that knowledge and education is truly "the most powerful weapon, which you can use to change the world," why do we treat educators this way?[15]

Furthermore, if the point of education is learning, why does it seem like testing drives everything? To the point where testing often obstructs learning, instead of supporting it? According to education and creativity expert Ken Robinson, this obsession with testing has unintentionally created a culture of compliance where "our children and teachers are encouraged to follow routine algorithms rather than to excite that power of imagination and curiosity."[16]

And why are we still teaching students how to become compliant factory workers, when our world is changing so rapidly? Instead of solving math problems for math's sake, what would happen if students were challenged to build model bridges, where math was required to get the job done? Rather than writing a generic book report, what if students learned how to write a marketing brief on the book instead? And instead of memorizing history, what if students walked through the steps of starting a business by solving a historical problem in a contemporary way?

It's encouraging to see educational leaders, school administrators, teachers, and entrepreneurs in today's gig economy trying to solve these problems. Many are trying to do something to address the systemic issues in our education system because they've realized that knowledge alone is not enough.

A few years ago, entrepreneur and freelancer Adam Braun ventured on his second start-up to reform education—this time focusing on post-secondary education. He started MissionU to create a debt-free alternative to prepare high school graduates with the right skills, knowledge, and education to succeed in today's most demanding jobs and companies. If you were accepted into the program, there was no up-front tuition cost. It was only after you found a job where you were making $50,000 or more annually that you would be required to pay back a percentage of your income for thirty-six months.

So instead of your degree (and corresponding student debt) being the credential used to help get you a job, employable skills and recent work experience become more valuable. That's why the final trimester of the program included a fellowship where you would work with companies like Spotify, Lyft, Uber, Warby Parker, Harry's, and Casper.[17]

He must've been onto something because after a couple years into his experiment, the $20-billion start-up WeWork acquired MissionU. While the coworking space company,

WeWork, technically doesn't have anything to do with education, the spouse of its cofounder and CEO does.

In the fall of 2017, Rebekah Neumann founded WeGrow to educate and raise "conscious global citizens of the world, to understand their passions, and know how to use those gifts to help others."[18] After their pilot year, they opened up their first expression of WeGrow as an elementary school in New York City for forty students. In addition to covering the standard subjects, students learn Hebrew and Mandarin, as well as how to cook using the food that they're growing on a farm. They engage with the arts, have weekly immersion experiences in nature, and are mentored by creators and experts in a variety of fields.[19]

According to WeGrow's FAQ page and based on the fact that they acquired MissionU and hired its founder to be their COO, it doesn't look like they're going to be just focusing on elementary education. And with both Neumann and Braun at the helm, it'll be exciting to see what they come up with as they try to reinvent the education system.

By no means is this the only example of an attempt to reform the education system. Plenty of individuals and organizations are working hard to improve the way young people are educated and formed. And while I'm grateful for all the entrepreneurs who are trying to reinvent the broken education system, I'm not convinced that any of their current models will make a significant dent. After all, how do they ever expect to go beyond Coleman's report where parents have to pay at least $35,000 per year per child to experience a different kind of education? It just sounds like history is on repeat, and that socioeconomic segregation is alive and well.

The Endless Pursuit of Knowledge

If knowledge was the silver bullet to achieving the American Dream, then shouldn't the most educated be our role models? Wouldn't they be the ones that have it all and are living the good life? What's ironic is that the more you *know* about a specific subject, the more you realize just how much you *don't know* about everything else—just ask someone with a PhD.

After living a life devoted to examining and exploring all things under heaven, King Solomon had this to say about the pursuit of knowledge.

> I said to myself, "See, I have amassed wisdom far beyond all those who were over Jerusalem before me, and my mind has thoroughly grasped wisdom and knowledge." I applied my mind to know wisdom and knowledge, madness and folly; I learned that this too is a pursuit of the wind. For with much wisdom is much

sorrow; as knowledge increases, grief increases. (Eccles. 1:16–18)

Solomon is not saying that we should live in ignorance or take Pol Pot's approach to knowledge and education. Just consider some of his proverbs on knowledge, "The wise store up knowledge, but the mouth of the fool hastens destruction" (Prov. 10:14). "Whoever loves discipline loves knowledge, but one who hates correction is stupid" (Prov. 12:1). "The inexperienced inherit foolishness, but the sensible are crowned with knowledge" (Prov. 14:18). And "a wise warrior is better than a strong one, and a man of knowledge than one of strength" (Prov. 24:5).

Clearly, Solomon is not dismissing the importance of knowledge. He's just helping us understand what happens when we make the pursuit of knowledge our life's goal.

So let's say, just for a moment, that you do make this your goal. You ignore Solomon, and see yourself through the lens of this lie that you are what you know. What do you think would happen?

If the pursuit of knowledge drives everything in your life, you might get accepted into an Ivy League school. Upon graduating, you might win a full ride to Oxford as a Rhodes scholar. And then, to continue learning, you might spend your money curating a collection of books that even librarians would be in awe of. And then what? Do you get multiple doctorates? What would you do with them? Or maybe, when you start working, you realize that your boss doesn't even know half of what you know, yet he's making double your salary! Then what?

No matter how accomplished you become as a result of your knowledge, you will eventually arrive at the same place Solomon did: it never ends and it's never enough. Pursuing knowledge as an end in and of itself, or as a means to the American Dream, is like chasing the wind. It's like trying to stop a leaky corroded pipe with the tip of a sharp pencil. Sure, it will stop the water for a moment, but it'll only be a matter of time until it bursts again, or another section of the pipe starts leaking.

Conclusion

A couple years ago, Lee Sedol and AlphaGo faced off in a historic Go match where the thirty-seventh move made history. If you're not familiar with the game, Go is "an abstract strategy board game for two players, in which the aim is to surround more territory than the opponent."[20] Think chess, but on a larger board, and exponentially more complex.

The reason this match was so historical was not just because the world's best Go player lost to a machine made by DeepMind—something that wasn't projected to happen for another ten years—but because of the thirty-seventh move.

When AlphaGo, which is DeepMind's artificially intelligent (A.I.) machine, made the thirty-seventh move in the match's second game, everyone thought it was a mistake. In fact, it took Lee Sedol nearly fifteen minutes to figure out his next move because it took him by surprise—the move just didn't make sense . . . to a human.

But to AlphaGo, it made perfect sense. This machine learned how to play by being fed thirty million moves from expert players. Then, through reinforcement learning, AlphaGo played countless matches against itself whereby it learned new strategies and grew its neural network. DeepMind then collected this information and fed it into a second neural network that would allow AlphaGo to anticipate the potential results of each move. "So AlphaGo learns from human moves, and then it learns from moves made when it plays itself. It understands how humans play, but it can also look beyond how humans play to an entirely different level of the game."[21]

In other words, AlphaGo knew so much about the game, and anticipated what was about to happen based on the previous thirty-six moves, that it made a move that no human would've ever made. A machine advanced a 2,500-year-old game beyond human knowledge.

What's sobering is that, today, there are A.I. machines that know more facts than we do—beating out the best *Jeopardy* contestants.[22] And if A.I. continues to progress at the rate it's been growing, there's no telling what could be next—especially if put in the wrong hands.

After all, how should we feel when Shane Legg, who is the cofounder and chief scientist of DeepMind, thinks "human extinction will probably occur, and technology will likely play a part in this." Heck, even the innovative, forward-thinking, rocket-launching, self-driving-car making, tech giant Elon Musk believes that we have the potential to produce "a fleet of artificial intelligence-enhanced robots capable of destroying mankind." Perhaps this is why he cofounded OpenAI, a billion-dollar nonprofit company, to work toward safer artificial intelligence.[23]

A.I., reinventing education, and the pursuit of knowledge—none of these are worth building your life upon. The endless pursuit of knowledge, it turns out, is just another way to chase the wind.

Chapter 5

Hoarders "R" Us

Trashalanche!

That's what Ryland's dad calls the sound of garbage tumbling off a mountain of junk. What's unfortunate is that the landfill isn't outside of their home—the landfill is *in* their home.[1]

Sixteen-year-old Grace, on the other hand has gotten used to it. As a child, she would have to climb over piles of clothes and shoes to get to the computer in the corner of their living room. Occasionally she would make it without causing a trashalanche, but more often than not, stuff would fall and the piles would spread.[2]

But at least Grace has a bed to sleep in. Randy's bed is literally a blanket that he lays down on top of his stuff. In the middle of his bedroom, in between mountains of old lamps, boxes, newspapers, computer monitors, filing cabinets, and his dresser, is his makeshift bed. When asked about his sleeping arrangements, he said, "It's uncomfortable at first, but you kind of get used to it after a while."[3]

And then there's Gary . . . oh, Gary. Gary was upset that his neighbors reported him. He couldn't believe that they wouldn't mind their own business. I mean, if he wants to sleep in his front yard, keep his clothes and most prized possessions there, and have his food all piled up in small mountains, isn't that his prerogative? What does that have to do with any of his neighbors? It's not like Gary's homeless and is just squatting in front of an abandoned home. This is *his* home! So why does he sleep and keep so much of his possessions out front? You guessed it. It's because the inside of his house is so full of stuff that he's run out of space—for himself.[4]

We're All Hoarders . . . to Some Extent

Over the past decade, real stories like these have moved our awareness of hoarding from the margins to the mainstream. After all, when you watch reality shows like A&E's *Hoarders*, it's hard to ignore what's going on. As a point of reference, this show debuted in 2009 to 2.5 million viewers and ran for nine seasons.[5] And by no means is this show the only one out there. The documentary *World of Compulsive Hoarders* preceded A&E's show in 2007, and TLC's *Hoarding* along with other related shows have come

after, including Netflix's *Tidying Up with Marie Kondo.*
Oprah even covered the lives of hoarders in two separate
episodes on her talk show.

Now there's even a thing called digital hoarding. Just
look up "Millennial Hoarders | The New Yorker" on
YouTube and you'll see what I'm talking about.

Are you a hoarder? If you're comparing yourself to the
hoarders on TV, probably not. But have you ever considered
that you just might have the symptoms to become one? Here
are a few diagnostic questions you can ask yourself.

Do you have things you haven't used in years but can't
seem to throw away because you *might* use them one day?
When you look at your closet, how many of your clothes
are just sitting there not being worn—either because you're
wanting to wear it again when you lose a few pounds, or
because you're hoping it comes back in fashion one day? Do
you have piles of magazines, newspapers, or books that keep
tipping over? Do your children sleep with a lot of items on
their bed? Do you like collecting free things, or enjoy shopping at thrift stores for deals? Do you have trouble making
decisions, organizing, or categorizing? Is your computer
desktop cluttered with icons, folders, and files? Is your email
inbox never at zero? Is your Netflix watch list so long that
it'll take you months to get through it?

Why Is Hoarding a Thing?

Before we move on, let's clarify what and whom we're talking about because exhibiting symptoms for hoarding and having a hoarding disorder are two very different things. For the rest of this chapter, when I talk about hoarding, I am not addressing those who struggle with hoarding disorder, which is in the DSM-5 (a manual of disorders for psychologists). I am not referring to the 4 to 5 percent of the population in most Western countries afflicted with this disorder.[6]

Rather, when I talk about hoarding, I'm focusing on the rest of us, who may have answered positively to a few of those previously listed questions. I'm referring to those who might have a messy house, possibly live amidst *organized* clutter, and occasionally get called a "pack rat."

And if that's not you, you likely live with or at least know someone who fits the criteria.

In fact, immediately after writing that last section, my wife and I went on a rampage to clear out the clutter from our house. We didn't Marie Kondo everything by asking whether or not the item "sparked joy" before throwing it away, like the popular Japanese organizing consultant and author suggests. Rather, we just threw away all the extra. Christina threw away dead plants and helped our kids clean up their rooms. And I got rid of two bags worth of clothes from my closet that I hadn't worn in a couple years.

Why do we do it? Why do we let stuff accumulate? Why do we hoard? Do we really have that much discretionary cash? Is our obsession for more the reason Black Friday has been extended from a day to a week? Is this also why Amazon has now moved from two-day shipping to same-day shipping and, in some cases, two-hour delivery? To get our stuff to us faster, so that we have another reason to order again?

Or, is the reason we hoard because we've come to believe the lie that's been fed to us? That we are what we own?

Lie #5: You Are What You Own

The first rule of Fight Club is? Do you know the answer? If not, try typing it into Google and see what comes up.

Whether you've seen the highly controversial cult classic or not, *Fight Club* is regarded as one of the greatest films of the 1990s, and to many, of all time.[7]

I wonder why? I doubt it's because of the twist at the end, though that was shocking. And it definitely could've done without a few scenes, but it's Hollywood, so what else would you expect?

At the beginning of the film, the unnamed narrator looks like a lost puppy trying to find his way home. He's at a dead-end job, struggling with insomnia, and living as "a slave to the IKEA nesting instinct." While flipping through catalogues, he would ask himself, "What kind of dining set defines me as a person?"[8]

Life was uneventful, steady, and predictable for the narrator until the day he returned home from a business trip only to walk into a crime scene. If it wasn't bad enough that someone had set off an explosive in his apartment building, things went from bad to worse when he discovered that it was his specific apartment unit that was targeted. Not having anyone else to turn to, he calls up the soap salesman, Tyler Durden, whom he had just met on the flight home. And they decide to meet at a bar.

At the bar, the narrator sighs and starts lamenting about everything he's lost. His furniture, his stereo, his wardrobe—all his things. Not impressed with the pity party that's going on, Tyler bluntly responds by saying how the real problem in society isn't murder, crime, or poverty— it's actually consumerism. And in a moment of profound insight, Tyler points out that "the things you own end up owning you."[9]

We Hoard Because . . .

Here's the thing. We don't hoard for the sake of hoarding, or to get on TV shows where our lives are put under a microscope for all the world to see. We hoard because we've come to believe this lie that we are what we own.

This is why you can tell a lot about a person just by looking at their credit card statement. If you don't believe me, try this exercise. Grab a few friends, print out your credit card statements, cross out any details that might reveal anyone's identity, and then shuffle them up. If you're feeling adventurous, see if you can match up each statement with the right person. Or, if you're not ready to be *that* vulnerable with your friends, try to come up with a personality portrait for each credit card statement. Based on their purchases, what do they value? How do they spend their time? What kind of person are they?

It's shocking, but the way we spend our money surprisingly reflects what we value, who we think we are, and how we want to appear to others—more than we might be aware of or even be willing to admit.

So someone who buys a condo in the city is making a different statement than someone who purchases a home in the suburbs within a planned community. And someone who builds a tiny home has a different set of values than someone who buys a fixer-upper in a gentrifying neighborhood.

What about the car you drive? Isn't it a reflection of your personality too? After all, when's the last time you met someone who owned both a Tesla and a Ford F-350? Or, what about a person who drives a Honda Civic? How are they different from a person who drives a minivan, BMW, or Kia Soul? And now with the rise of the gig economy, what does it say about a person who buys a fuel-efficient car *so that* they can drive for Uber? Or better yet, perhaps because of Uber, they don't even buy a car at all?

Just think about your phone. Based on the amount of time you spend on it, how you feel if you've forgotten it somewhere, and what you do when you're on it—it's essentially become an extension of yourself. This means that the kind of person who always gets the newest iPhone every year is different from the one who is always a couple models behind.

The same can be said about your watch, souvenirs that you've collected over the years, and the stacks of books and magazines in your home, just to name a few. You can tell a lot about a person based on what they own.

Status, Value, and Being Rejected

We believe that we are what we own because our culture has infused status and value into material objects. However, there's a slight nuance that we need to pay attention to: what's important for me may not be important for you. In other words, while some of you might scoff at hoarders who see quantity as the *chief end of man,* chasing quality or the "right" things isn't necessarily any better. And by "right," I'm referring to things that you believe will elevate your social status and class, rather than things that might be more functional.

No wonder compulsive hoarders look like they're having a mental breakdown when family and friends arrive with a trash bag. The objects that they've hoarded are not just static material *things* without any meaning—they are extensions of themselves. So when their stuff gets thrown away, it's like they're being thrown away. This is why hoarders react so emotionally during a cleanup—they feel rejected and disposed of by the very people who are supposed to love them the most.

This is also why—if you chase after quality or the "right" things—you might flip out if someone scratches your car, if you crack the screen on your phone, or if a sentimental necklace goes missing. Your emotional reaction is a compass that points to what you value and just how much you value it.

As a result, even if you're not a compulsive hoarder, I hope you're beginning to see how the things you own are reflections and extensions of yourself—your beliefs, your values, and how you want to appear to others.

~~You Are What You Own~~

Is this why people have turned to minimalism? And why Marie Kondo has sold millions of books and has her own show on Netflix? Is it because we are trying to find a way to escape the rat race?

I recently came across a fascinating documentary on minimalism. It follows two guys who were climbing the corporate ladder and living for their paychecks. Disillusioned with what that was getting them, they decided to quit their full-time jobs and start freelancing and gigging in hopes of a better life. Here's what one of them said:

> I had everything I ever wanted. I had everything I was supposed to have. Everyone around me said, "You're successful." But really, I was miserable. There was this gaping hole in my life. So I tried to fill that void the same way many people do—with stuff, lots of stuff.... I was spending money faster than I was earning it, attempting to buy my way to happiness. I thought I'd get there one day. Eventually I mean, happiness had to be somewhere just around the corner. I was living paycheck to paycheck, living for a paycheck, living for stuff. But I wasn't living at all.[10]

These guys rejected the view that they are what they own by embracing minimalism. This means no more McMansions with three-car garages, granite countertops, bonus rooms, and a private pool. Or, to put it another way, no more shopping at Costco and IKEA to buy mass-produced goods and services. Essentially, minimalism requires you to reject the very thing that encourages the acquiring of stuff in ever increasing amounts—consumerism.

Although this documentary on minimalism was fascinating, and while it eventually led me to binge-watch shows on tiny homes, here's what stood out to me. Though these guys rejected the view that they are what they own, their minimalist lifestyles didn't make them seem any better off. Just because they weren't living for things didn't mean that they could live for free. They still needed money. So no, they didn't have a traditional 9 to 5 job with a boss anymore. And yes, they got to set their own work hours and determine their own workload, since they were freelancing and gigging. But they didn't actually seem any happier or more content.

Here's what neuropsychologist Rick Hanson says about minimalism, "I think it goes to the bottom line fact that you can never get enough of what you don't really want. In other words, deep down, we don't want more goodies, more toys, more cars. We want what they will bring us. We want to feel whole. We want to feel content."[11]

Acquiring more and more stuff can never leave you fulfilled because you are not what you own. However, getting rid of everything and trying to empty yourself doesn't seem to work either. So now what?

E-cards and Letters

It's fun to look back at the letters Christina and I wrote to each other while we were dating. If I were to take one of those letters, copy it word-for-word onto letterhead, and then hand it to her today, what do you think would happen? How would she react? Would it still make sense?

Here's an excerpt from the e-card I sent to her on February 14, 2005. Back then, when we were dating long distance, e-cards were cool . . . I think.

> Christina, I really am more in love with you than I have ever been and it seems like my love for you is growing with every passing moment. Through good times and bad, hasn't God really been shaping our character and our love for each other? I seriously wake up every day thanking God for you in my life. He has blessed us so much to give us each other at this age right now. Oh Christina, you really are the light of my life and there is a special place deep down in my heart that is only reserved for you. I am so overjoyed to know that you will take it.

Most of this would work. In fact, I'd probably get a lot of brownie points if I wrote this out on a *physical* card and gave it to her on Valentine's Day—until she came across the phrases "at this age right now," and "I am so overjoyed to know that you will take it."

With a curious look on her face, she'd point to these two phrases and ask me to clarify, "Daniel, what are you trying to say? I don't get it. Why are we blessed to have each other at this age *right now*? Were we not blessed before? Will we not be blessed later? And that place deep down inside of your heart . . . am I only now taking it? What about the past fourteen years that we've been married?!"

The thing is, when you divorce context from content, letters like this become one-dimensional. They go from being a heartfelt confession of love on our first Valentine's Day—seven months after we started dating long-distance— to mere platitudes that you might find on a cheesy greeting card.

The same thing is true with the letters in the Bible. When reading them, you need to keep in mind that they were letters written to specific groups of people at particular points in time. If you see them this way, and refuse to divorce context from content, an amazing thing happens. Not only will you better comprehend the original intended meaning of each letter, but you will also discover just how significant they can be to your life today. This is because, unlike other books, the Bible is the Word of God, which makes it "living and effective and sharper than any double-edged sword, penetrating as far as the separation of soul and spirit, joints and marrow. It is able to judge the thoughts and intentions of the heart" (Heb. 4:12).

So let's take a look at the letter Paul wrote to the Philippian church. In it, we'll see what he has to say about the lie that you are what you own.

> I have learned to be content in whatever circumstances I find myself. I know both how to make do with little, and I know how to make do with a lot. In any and all circumstances I have learned the secret of being content—whether well fed or hungry, whether in abundance or in need. I am able to do all things through him who strengthens me. (Phil. 4:11–13)

If anyone had the street cred to say he had learned the secret to contentment, it was Paul. He had the pedigree and all the right credentials. He was a religious leader in the day, educated by the best of the best, with a bright career ahead of him—but he decided to give it all up when he met Jesus.

And after meeting Jesus, he didn't walk the path of apathy. He went all in—so much so that he went from being the persecutor to the persecuted.

So when Paul said that he had learned the secret of being content in any and *all* circumstances, this is what he meant. Here's a *brief* list of the circumstances that he was referring to:

> Five times I received the forty lashes minus one from the Jews. Three times I was beaten with rods. Once I received a stoning. Three times I was shipwrecked. I have spent a night and a day in the open sea. On frequent journeys, I faced dangers from rivers, dangers from robbers, dangers from my own people, dangers from Gentiles, dangers in the city, dangers in the wilderness, dangers at sea, and dangers among false brothers; toil and hardship, many sleepless nights, hunger and thirst, often without food, cold, and without clothing. (2 Cor. 11:24–27)

If this list wasn't bad enough, when Paul told the Philippians he knew the secret to contentment, he was in prison! And it wasn't because he committed some injustice to humanity; he was in prison because he was telling others about the path to contentment. He was jailed for trying to help, not hurt.

When you refuse to divorce context from content, you realize that there's an extra layer of depth and credibility behind Paul's words. His words are not flat, one-dimensional platitudes that you might find on a greeting card. He has experienced the highs and lows of life, and everything in between. So when someone like this says that he's learned to be content in whatever circumstances he finds himself, it'd be foolish to look the other way, wouldn't it?

So, What Is It?

What, exactly, is the secret to contentment?

It's focus. The secret to contentment is focus. Let me use an analogy to explain.

Imagine you're flying over the Atlantic Ocean from Nashville to Iceland. And let's say that the GPS was broken and the autopilot wasn't working, so you had to fly the plane old-school. What are the chances that you'd fly on a straight path to Iceland, which is close to three thousand nautical miles away? If not, how far off course would you be?

To help calculate where you'd end up, pilots have a rule of thumb called the "1 in 60 rule" that they use to course correct when they're off track.[12] According to this rule, if you were flying off course by one degree starting from Nashville, after three thousand nautical miles you would end up approximately fifty nautical miles away from Iceland somewhere over the North Atlantic Ocean. Now as long as your plane had enough fuel, it wouldn't be too difficult to course correct, right? After all, you'd only have to make up fifty nautical miles.

But what if your plane was twenty degrees off course? After three thousand nautical miles, although you would still be somewhere over the North Atlantic Ocean, rather than just making a simple course correction, you'd be preparing for a descent into London's Heathrow Airport—close to one thousand nautical miles away from Iceland!

In life, just like flying, you don't move toward wishful thinking or plans on a piece of paper—no matter how well designed or thought out they are. You move in the direction you're focusing on. So if you notice Teslas everywhere you go and you can't seem to get enough of those home renovation shows, you simply won't feel content until you're charging your own Tesla and wiping down your new countertops.

But then what? What do you do when that feeling of contentment *eventually* goes away? You just set your focus on whatever's next—hoping that this time you will reach contentment, right? But when you don't, the cycle just goes on and on.

When your focus is on the things you own, contentment is as far away as the next undiscovered galaxy in space. You know it's probably there so you keep on searching for it. And when you discover it, you're happy; but when you realize that the presence of that galaxy means there are even more undiscovered galaxies out there, a sense of futility sets in. The same thing is true when you think contentment is achieved through emptying yourself. You'll never get rid of enough—and when you think you have, you'll meet someone else with even less.

After reading everything Paul wrote and examining the records of his life, I can't find any evidence that he bought or emptied his way to contentment. Instead, it appears that he may have actually just stumbled into it. Consider what he said earlier in his letter to the Philippian church.

> Not that I have already reached the goal or am already perfect, but I make every effort to take hold of it because I also have been taken hold of by Christ Jesus. Brothers and sisters, I do not consider myself to have taken hold of it. But one thing I do: Forgetting what is behind and reaching forward to what is ahead, I pursue as my goal the prize promised by God's heavenly call in Christ Jesus. (Phil. 3:12–14)

Being content is not about having everything figured out, nor is it about perfection. After all, the very man who said he had learned the secret of being content is the same one who wrote these words right here!

Here's how I think it all came together for Paul when he found the secret to being content. As Paul left behind his former life of living for stuff, and started living for Jesus—focusing on Jesus and following after him—he stumbled into contentment.

Think about it like this: imagine you've been cooped up in your home for the past three days because of the flu. You're not at 100 percent, but somehow your friend convinces you to go on a hike to get some fresh air. Hoping that going outside will make you feel better, you reluctantly agree, even though you can't remember the last time you ever *willingly* went hiking. As you start down the trail, you can't help but laugh as your friend catches you up on everything you've missed. With the sound of leaves crunching underneath your feet, you look up and realize that you're surrounded with the colors of autumn—hues of amber, crimson, chocolate, and magenta leaves everywhere. And just like that, almost in an instant, you realize that you're actually having a good time.

When you look back, you don't precisely know when the shift took place, but somewhere along the journey something changed. You started feeling better and you noticed that you were enjoying the hike. Instead of focusing on your lack of energy, or the fact that you had to bundle yourself up, pull out your runners, and drive an hour to the trail, your focus shifted—and that's when your heart changed.

That's what contentment is like. It's something you stumble into, and grow in over time, when your focus shifts to Jesus. This is because contentment is a direction, not a destination. It's an outcome, not an action. It's something that comes out of a slow cooker, not from a microwave. You can't click to download it—there's no button. You can't choose it, as if it were some sort of one-off decision that you could make in isolation. You can't positively think your way to contentment either, no matter how many times you chant it. It's simply not something you can just "add to your cart," or pull out of a vending machine.

So stop believing the lies. Self-help is not the answer to contentment. More or less stuff isn't the path to contentment either. If it were, then both the wealthy and the minimalists would've claimed success by now, but they haven't because contentment doesn't work that way.

The only path to contentment is through Jesus, since Jesus has already given and promised us *everything* we need—even though there's nothing we've done or can ever do to deserve it.

Conclusion

Years after Jack Whittaker won $315 million in the lottery, he told reporters that he wished he had torn up his ticket.

This is the same man who, before winning the lottery, would typically rise at 4:30 a.m. to get ready for work. Ever since Jack was a poor fourteen-year-old in West Virginia, he had been working in construction. And by the time he was fifty-five, through hard work and sweat equity, he was already a millionaire. Although he was living an enviable life to most as the president of a successful construction company that employed more than one hundred people, he never flaunted it. He lived a humble life with his wife and granddaughter in a modest brick home. But that morning when he discovered that he had the winning numbers, everything changed.

Overnight, he became Santa Claus. And with this new-found fame and fortune, he vowed to give away millions, build big new churches, and start a charitable foundation to help West Virginians. He even told one of the reporters, "I want to be a good example. I want to make people proud of what happens with this winning. I want to promote good-will and help people."

If giving away money is considered helping, then yes, I guess he helped people. But if helping people with money ultimately leads to people targeting him, breaking into his car, stealing his briefcases of cash, his granddaughter's death, and his wife divorcing him, then maybe Jack should've revisited his definition of that word. There's a kind of helping that actually helps, but then there's another kind that just ends up hurting you and everyone around you.

Jack had all the money he ever needed, but he wasn't content. And after the death of his granddaughter, here's what he said:

> My granddaughter is dead probably because of the money. I know I really had my arms around her and protected her before I won the lottery. But once I won the lottery, there wasn't enough of me to get my arms around everything—to hold her and protect her . . . I pretty much lost everything I had held dear in my life . . . I don't know where it'll end, but you know, I don't like Jack Whittaker. I don't like the hard heart I got. I just don't like what I've become.[13]

Wow. All this from a man who could've bought anything he dreamed of. I guess it's true that the things you own can ultimately end up owning you.

Chapter 6

It's Not about You

I'm going to be a YouTuber when I grow up."

No, I didn't say that—but it's not because I have something against YouTube. It just wasn't around when I was a child. Instead, I aspired to a more *modest* life as a professional hockey player. However, after painfully realizing that my road hockey skills didn't quite translate onto the ice, I decided to go for Plan B—becoming a K-Pop star.

I guess I've always liked being in the limelight, but since I didn't live in Korea, there was pretty much zero chance of that dream ever coming true. It's not like I could've just filmed a video of myself on my Samsung flip phone and then uploaded it to the Internet for everyone to see. And let's say my parents had let me use their camcorder; how did you even get videos onto the Internet before YouTube, and share them with friends without Facebook?

For Filipino-Canadian Elle Mills, it was a different story. As a child, all she ever did was make videos. And though she likely didn't realize the impact it would have on her until much later in life, her seventh birthday present changed everything for her. I wonder if she's ever thanked the three cofounders of YouTube for creating the video-sharing website in 2005—because without it, Elle Mills, as we know her to be today, would not exist.

Becoming a YouTuber was her dream, and everyone around her knew it. In high school, she was voted by her peers most likely to be a YouTuber, and upon graduation, she made a promise to herself that she was going to do it. She was so serious about achieving this dream, that she even dropped out of university to "try the YouTube thing" after realizing that she couldn't keep up with both her grades and her rapidly growing YouTube channel.[1]

Once she hit one million subscribers on YouTube, she invited a few of her friends and family to her "graduation from irrelevancy" to celebrate this accomplishment—and obviously capture it all for YouTube. Here's what she said to set up the video, "I've always said, don't let the numbers define you. But then again, that was before I hit one million subscribers. So sure I still live at home with my mom, and still don't know how to cook. And I might be in debt, but at least now I'm relevant."[2]

Elle Mills had officially made it as a YouTuber. One of her videos went viral with over four million views. She won the 10th annual Shorty Award for Breakout YouTuber. She started speaking at conventions. And the legendary YouTuber, Casey Neistat, even gave her a shout-out on one of his videos. Here's what he said about her:

> Every once in a while, there's a unicorn. That is, someone I see on YouTube who just like blows my mind. A creator doing something so new and so fresh that it makes me question my own creativity. Because it's not just a new take on an existing genre. It's not just doing the same thing other people are doing, but better. It's completely new from every perspective. So this is me talking about my new favorite YouTuber. Her name is ElleoftheMills.[3]

YouTuber: The New Career

Elle had become a YouTuber—the very thing that 34 percent of children aged six to seventeen recently said they were aspiring to be when they grew up.[4] A separate study of children aged seven to eleven confirmed this newfound aspiration, and it revealed that becoming a YouTuber was surprisingly more desirable than a career as an actor or a pop singer.[5]

So if you're a parent, it's time to face the facts: you'll never be able to impress your children's friends on "Bring Your Parent to School Day" unless you have your own YouTube channel. Apparently being a firefighter, pilot, or doctor isn't as cool as it used to be.

If this is blowing your mind, try asking your friends whether they know a child who wants to be a YouTuber when they grow up—the majority will say yes. And while some children are aspiring to be YouTubers because they think it means they'll get paid to play video games, get free toys, or because they've heard it's an easy way to make money—there are many children who want to do it for creative control, fame, and self-expression.[6]

Even university professors are recognizing the legitimacy of this newfound career path. Damian Salas, assistant dean of Drexel University's Entrepreneurship Programs, just hopes future YouTubers won't neglect getting a college degree, since "there's the business side of the YouTube model that students need to have more education about." In an interview with NBC News, he told the reporter, "Sure, you can create a YouTube channel, but to grow the YouTube channel, to scale it, and to really understand all the aspects of having a business that is centered around a YouTube channel is something that students and individuals need to understand."[7]

You Don't Need to Wait

The thing about being a YouTuber is that you don't have to grow up to be one. You can start your career as a pre-schooler like Ryan did when his parents set up a YouTube channel for him. Just a few years after launching his channel, he's been able to amass more than 22 million subscribers, with some of his videos garnering over one billion views. In 2018, he apparently earned over $22 million, which made him the highest-paid YouTuber in the world—and he was only eight years old at the time![8] If you still don't know which Ryan I'm referring to, you likely don't have a little one at home. I'm talking about the little boy from the YouTube channel, "Ryan ToysReview," where he literally *just* plays with toys.

Other popular child YouTubers play video games, share kid life hacks, or conduct science experiments. Some have been YouTubers for nearly their entire life, like Annie LeBlanc, who has received close to four million views on her channel since it launched over a decade ago—when she was three years old. Though that might seem impressive, it's actually nothing compared to the 3.6 billion views that her family has received on the channel they run together.

Then there are the ones who become so viral, like JoJo Siwa, that they get picked up by Nickelodeon Kids for a multiplatform deal that includes original programming, social media, live events, music, and merchandise. And that merchandise is not just referring to JoJo's famous bows. According to the press release, it will include "apparel, home furnishings, toys, accessories, publishing and more."[9]

Thanks to the rising gig economy, becoming a YouTuber has become a legitimate career choice. Instead of simply being a platform to consume and share the latest viral cat video, prank video, or trending music video, an increasing number of individuals are seeing it as a viable place to produce content and earn a living.

Just consider the fact that over the past five years, YouTube has paid out more than $2 billion of advertising revenue to YouTubers. And when you look at their numbers, it's astonishing to see that the number of channels earning five figures per year is growing by more than 50 percent year over year![10] YouTube is quickly moving from being a hobby to replacing your day job—and it's all thanks to this new normal.

But here is what's adding fuel to the fire. Combined with TV and movies, YouTube has become the number-one influencer for children's career choices. This means that media is now influencing what our children want to be when they grow up, *more so than* their own personal passion or the influence of their parents and schools.[11]

I wonder about the long-term implications of this trend. Now if your children are watching *Doc McStuffins*, *Magic School Bus*, *Design Squad*, or *Project MC²*, I guess it's not all that bad. Shows like these are educational *and* entertaining. But what if they're watching *Caillou*, *SpongeBob*, or any of the toy review channels on YouTube? How do you think shows like these are influencing them? In their career choices, character development, sense of contentment, and other things that really matter in life?

On top of all that, is there something to learn from the rising number of high profile YouTubers burning out, taking a break, or quitting altogether? Do they know something we don't about what happens as you go deeper and deeper into making a career out of being a YouTuber? And if some of the most successful YouTubers are burning out, why would we let them influence and mentor our children—which we're essentially doing when we let our children watch them?

Passive Parenting

When's the last time you handed your phone to your child? Not to make a call, or look up directions somewhere, but just so that they'd be quiet or stop making a scene? I'm trying to do this less, but honestly, it's been my default reaction for years—and it all started with restaurants.

Early in our marriage when we couldn't afford babysitting and our children were toddlers, Christina and I would often bring them along on our dates to restaurants. Depending on the day, our meals at home were either focused on entertaining the kids, or just making it through without spilling something. So on date night, things had to look and feel different—well, at least we had to try.

To facilitate this *romantic* evening, we'd hand our phones or an iPad to our children to occupy them. It was brilliant. Instant babysitting. The kids loved it because they could watch as much as they wanted to. And for us, it actually felt like a date, since we could talk and neither of us had to clean up afterward.

I wish I could tell you that I vetted and prewatched everything they consumed, but I didn't. Now obviously they weren't watching *The Walking Dead,* or some sketchy show with mature content. But beyond the surface level of age-appropriate TV parental guidelines, I had no idea what messages my children were being subliminally fed through these shows.

And subliminally being fed they were! Let me illustrate through a game. Try matching the left and right sides together—the worldview and message that the show is propagating on the one side, and the name of the show on the other.[12]

Life is better with more toys.	Caillou
I'm going to whine until I get my own way.	
	Bill Nye the Science Guy
It's okay to lie to your parents, as long as you come home for dinner.	
	Cat in the Hat
Be random and do whatever you want— just do it with friends.	
	Sponge Bob Square Pants
Everything can and must be explained by Science, otherwise it's not true.	
	Ryan's Toy Review

Scary, isn't it?

Now, don't get me wrong. I'm not saying that you need to become a Luddite and destroy all access points to the media. I'm simply trying to make the connection for you between the research and everyday life. If media, which includes YouTube, has become the number-one influencer for our children's career choices, what are the implications?

Now I get that parenting is tough, tiring, and often thankless, but if it's true that we reap what we sow, shouldn't we be paying more attention to what our children are watching? Instead of being passive, what if we tried to be more active in our parenting? And instead of being reactive, what if we were proactive?

Lie #6: You Are Who You Raise

Whenever I connect with new parents, it's fun (and stressful) to think back and remember what it was like for Christina and me. As new parents, we thought we could plan and prepare for everything—absolutely everything.

We were living in Seoul, South Korea, at the time, and someone suggested that we go to some baby fair/expo to learn everything we needed to know about being parents. Apparently, it was something parents did, so we just took their advice and went. While it was definitely educational in some respects, it wasn't in the way that we were initially thinking. Since none of the seminars were in English (I wonder if they would've just been product pitches anyway), we basically walked around the convention center for what seemed like hours. It was like a vortex. There were so many people, and an untold number of vendors, that I literally lost my sense of direction in there.

Instead of walking out confident, equipped, and prepared to raise a child, we left with a stroller, a UV sterilizer, and a lot of questions. We were definitely going to breastfeed . . . but what if Christina couldn't? There was no question our baby was going to sleep on her back . . . or was it her tummy? And we were obviously going to use disposable diapers . . . I think. And don't even ask me which carrier or wrap we were going to use.

Eventually we settled into a manageable rhythm. We were beginning to sleep at night and feel pretty confident in our ability to parent—and then our second child was born fifteen months later. Just because something worked for our first daughter didn't mean that it was going to work for our second one, and vice versa. And then, three years later we had a boy—who *still* needs help getting to sleep.

Parenting is tiring, isn't it? The sleepless nights—either because you have a newborn that needs your help, or a teen that refuses to listen—on top of the inertia of life, are just two of the many reasons we drift into rhythms and routines. It often seems like the only way to survive! I believe Thomas Jefferson put it best when he said, "We hold these Truths to be self-evident, that all Men are created equal . . . *and live and die by their habits.*"

Okay, maybe that's not *quite* the way he put it, but nonetheless, you get the point. There's even research that discovered "40 percent of the actions people perform each day weren't actual decisions, but habits."[13] Why do you think Steve Jobs wore the same clothes every day, and Charles Dickens took three-hour walks every afternoon? Or how about the man famous for the Peanuts comic strips, Charles

Schultz? Why do you think he had a ham sandwich and glass of milk almost every day for lunch?[14]

It's because we are creatures of habit.

While you can probably identify your daily routines and habits in certain areas, you likely aren't aware of the extent to which they drive and govern your life. So yes, you probably shower, brush your teeth, and put on your shoes in a certain order, but what about the way that you deal with conflict? Relax? Express love? Or parent? Do you know why you do what you do?

What makes all of this even more complicated is that the older we get, the harder it is to change. So the end result is that we drift. We end up sinking into the habits, routines, patterns, or *normals* of life. In other words, we slip from intentionality to laziness. From being proactive to being reactive. From action to passivity.

And then one day we realize that we have no idea why we are doing what we're doing. And when it comes to parenting, that's a scary place to be.

Why We Do What We Do

I love my mom—I really do—but I could never understand why she would go through all that effort to make me drink carrot juice. It's not like I made it easy for her either. She had to fight tooth and nail with me before I'd drink that nasty concoction. And have you ever used an old-school juicer? It's a pain to clean up.

So why did she do it? Was she that concerned with my eyes? That I would rack up expensive optometry bills? That I would suddenly lose my vision, even though our family doesn't have a history of vision loss? Or, was there something else? Something beneath the surface that was driving her behavior—at an unconscious level?

To discover why we do what we do—especially as it relates to parenting—let's take an inside look into the life of Tiger Woods. Not Tiger the cheater, the philanthropist, or the golfer, but Tiger the son—Eldrick Tont "Tiger" Woods.

When Tiger turned pro in 1996, his father, Earl Woods, said something peculiar. Mind you, the spotlight was supposed to be on Tiger—Tiger's hard work, Tiger's accomplishments, and the fact that Tiger was going to become a multimillionaire overnight through endorsement deals with Nike and Titleist. However, as you'll shortly see, the reason Earl's words sounded so peculiar was because, underneath the surface, they were actually more about him than they were about Tiger. In fact, when you look at the way Earl and Kultida raised Tiger, things *always* seemed to be more about Earl than they were ever about Tiger. Tiger was simply the platform that Earl had built to stand on.

Here's the peculiar thing that Earl said when Tiger turned pro: "Tiger will do more than any other man to change the course of humanity." He will have a greater impact on humanity than Nelson Mandela, Gandhi, or Buddha "because he has a larger forum than any of them. Because he's playing a sport that's international. Because he's qualified through his ethnicity to accomplish miracles. He's the bridge between the East and the West. There is no limit because he has the guidance. I don't know yet exactly what form this will take. But he is the Chosen One. He'll have the power to impact nations. Not people. Nations. The world is just getting a taste of his power."[15]

The "Chosen One"? "Power"? "Nations"? Sure, I get that Tiger is one of the most accomplished athletes in history—he even topped ESPN's list of the twenty most dominant athletes of the past twenty years.[16] And yes, he has an aura to him that many have coined the "Tiger Effect," where he consistently boosts TV ratings every time he plays.[17] But no matter how proud you might be for your child, it takes some level of pompous bravado to say the things that Earl said. To call your child the "Chosen One"? Earl had to be overcompensating for something.

The elder Woods was determined to raise the world's greatest golfer. It was going to happen, no matter what. In fact, Earl was so convinced in *his own* ability to do so, that he even told others that God had personally selected him to nurture and raise Tiger.

Now it's hard to imagine Earl as a narcissistic, deadbeat, and absentee father who—as a serial adulterer and sex addict—cheated on both of his wives. No, *creepy old guy* is probably not the first thing that comes to mind when you think about Earl Woods. Rather, you probably remember him from that iconic embrace after Tiger sank his final putt to win the 1997 Masters. In the most-watched golf broadcast in US history, an estimated forty-three million viewers witnessed Earl as the perfect father who gave up everything so that his son could have it all.[18]

But Tiger, Kultida, and everyone else that Earl had used to advance his own agenda knew a different side to Earl—his real self. Earl was a different man behind the scenes.

Something else, beneath the surface, drove his behavior and the way he parented at an unconscious level. It certainly wasn't faith—even though he acted as if an angel had visited him and prophesied that his son was going to be the next savior of the world. Rather, it was his childhood. In particular, it was the fact that he never became the professional athlete that his father had always wanted him to become.

Growing up, Earl loved spending time with his elderly father at the minor league baseball stadium in town. Though his father was a stonemason by trade, the baseball stadium was where his father came alive. His father knew everything about every baseball player that came through the town. Baseball was his father's obsession, and nothing would have made his father prouder than for Earl to play in the major leagues.[19]

Earl knew this, and as an eleven-year-old dealing with the death of his father, he made his father's dream his own by resolving that he would make it to the pros. He was going to fulfill his father's last wish—and nothing was going to get in his way.

Unfortunately, being one of the best players on a very bad team wasn't enough to cut it—so his baseball career never advanced beyond college.[20] For the rest of his life, the shame of failing to fulfill his father's dream would haunt him—until an army buddy introduced him to golf. "If golf were a drug, he would have qualified as an addict. He liked it so much that it consumed him, leading him to spend far more time with his clubs than with his wife. 'I realized what I'd been missing my whole life,' Earl said. 'I decided if I had another son, I'd introduce him to golf early on.'"[21]

And this he certainly did. Except *introduce* probably isn't the right word to describe the way Earl approached golf with his son. After Tiger was born, Earl resolved to avoid repeating the mistakes that he had made with his children from his first marriage. He was going to get things right this time and be actively involved in his child's life. (Although I'm not quite sure how hitting golf balls into a net in your garage, while your six-month-old just watches you from his high chair, qualifies as being actively involved. Nor does it seem normal for a child to have a putter as his security blanket.[22])

Rather than *introduce*, Earl was grooming his son to be the athlete Earl never was. What else would explain a two-year-old spending two hours a day at the driving range with his dad? Or a father asking the local CBS affiliate in Los Angeles to do a story on his son? Or Tiger, as a two-year-old, appearing on the most popular daytime television talk show in all of America? Earl had an agenda for Tiger, and nothing was going to get in his way.

While Earl—likely unconsciously—was raising Tiger to be a professional athlete to deal with the shame he had from failing to fulfill his father's dream, Kultida had her own reasons for going along with it all. As a child in Thailand, she was neglected by her parents. She had to fend for herself, so becoming the kind of mother she never had drove everything for her. "That meant she would never rely on child care or work outside the home, no matter how stressed the family finances became. She would personally teach her son to read and write and multiply and divide. For her, it was simple: She was dedicating her life to her only child. Her boy would know he was loved."[23]

Earl and Kultida parented the way they did because— underneath the surface—they believed the lie that you are who you raise. Parenting was their opportunity to deal with their own junk—their unresolved hurt, shame, and regret from childhood. For Earl, Tiger turning pro would make up for the fact that he never became a professional athlete. And for Kultida, being with Tiger wherever he went would make up for the fact that she was neglected as a child. If Tiger won, Earl won. And if Tiger felt loved, Kultida felt loved.

Whether they realized it or not, they weren't ultimately parenting with Tiger in mind; they were parenting with themselves in mind.

~~You Are Who You Raise~~

This lie is so dangerous because it deceives you into believing that parenting ought to be your all and everything. That your children should be the center of your universe. After all, have you ever heard or seen this narrative before? "You're not sacrificing for your kids and giving them a chance at a better life? Wow . . ."

Or how about this one, "She's smart like her mother, and hardworking like me, but what we love most about our daughter is the fact that she never gives up."

What do you think would happen if their daughter decided to take a break from competitive sports? And started slacking off at school? Would the parents pressure her to try harder for her sake, or for their reputation? Is it that she never gives up? Or that her parents won't let her give up?

Or, what do you think would happen if you don't go to all of those mommy/daddy and me playtimes? Don't enroll your children in all of those extracurricular activities? And don't go on a college tour with your high school junior? When your child ends up flunking out of college and working a minimum-wage job for the rest of his life, you'll be the one to blame, right?

And think about the last time you drove behind someone who had one of those "My child is an honors student" bumper stickers. Why do parents stick these on their car? Who does it benefit the most? The child who doesn't drive? Or the parent who now has a way of signaling their own virtue as a model caregiver?

Do you see how deceptive this lie is? How subtle it can be? And the extent that it is *already* unconsciously governing your life and the way that you parent? On the surface, this lie doesn't seem too bad, since involvement in your child's life is better than neglect. However, underneath the surface, this lie actually tricks you into believing that your self-worth is tied directly to the performance of your children—and this is especially heightened for stay-at-home parents. No wonder pageant moms and overbearing soccer dads are a thing.

In other words, this lie that you are who you raise frauds you into believing that your children's success is your success. And their failure is your failure. No wonder Earl and

Kultida sacrificed everything for Tiger to win—even their marriage. Tiger was their everything. To put it another way, eerily, they were Tiger and Tiger was them.

Pride, Narcissism, and Control

At the root of this lie is pride. It's the belief that *you* are the one who is ultimately in control over the destiny of your children. It's the belief that you can shape and mold them into your image and likeness—that you have not only created them but can sustain them.

Joseph Burgo, in his excellent book on the rise of narcissism, advocates that individuals who parent in this manner are actually exploiting their children for narcissistic gain.[24] Raising *perfect* children becomes a new avenue for the proud or narcissistic to inflate their sense of self-importance and feel better about themselves. It's a new mountain to conquer, or avenue to seek contentment. And for narcissistic individuals who are dealing with the shame of unfulfilled dreams, like Earl, parenthood ends up becoming a second chance at life.

I hope you're noticing the foolishness of living according to this lie and defining yourself based on your children—and the amount of unnecessary and unrealistic pressure that it puts on you and your children. I also hope you're recognizing that it's actually arrogance, or an inflated sense of self-importance, that causes someone to even believe in this lie in the first place.

However, if these two reasons aren't enough to convince you to lay down this lie and walk the path of true contentment, as I shared in the last chapter, then how about we play this out to the end? Let's consider how parenting according to this lie affects your children.

What about the Children?

While you might remember a time when freelancing, gigging, and having a side hustle was out of the ordinary, for children today, it's just ordinary. They don't know any different. The gig economy just is—it's normal, not new. Unfortunately, this also means that for the average child, the lies that we've explored in this book will not even seem like lies.

If it's hard enough for adults to resist these lies, how much more so for children who don't know any different? *Especially* children who are being raised by prideful parents who believe that their self-worth, self-esteem, identity, or meaning in life is all tied into the success of the children they raise.

Just think about it. If a child grows up in an environment where *success* is defined by their parents, will the child ever feel accepted just as they are? For just being, and not doing? And what if the child succeeds at something that he or she is passionate about, but that his or her parents never cared for? How do you think self-centered, prideful, or narcissistic parents will react?

Underneath the surface, children who grow up with prideful parents that believe this lie will never feel accepted just as they are. Their parents will always drive them to succeed—often at things the kids never even originally chose for themselves. And it is only after they succeed at the things that matter most to their parents, that they will finally experience acceptance and love from their parents.

Consider Tiger. As a child, since his dad was obsessed with golf, playing the sport was the only way to virtually guarantee time with and attention from his dad. But starting from when Tiger was a preteen, rather than using encouraging words to build up his self-confidence during practice, Earl would tear him down and verbally abuse him to try to toughen him up. In 2017, Tiger later admitted that Earl had trained him to be "a 'cold-blooded assassin' on the course, by applying more of the principles he had learned and used while in the military."[25]

I get that there are times where tough love is necessary, but doesn't every child ultimately need to experience unconditional love and affection from his or her parents? Regardless of what they do, how they perform, or how much they might mess up? Maybe Earl's method helped Tiger win more tournaments, but what do you think it did to his sense of identity and self-worth when he realized that winning was the only road to his dad's heart? And how directly did it then cultivate a narcissistic, addictive, and obsessive personality in Tiger that, like a time bomb, kept on ticking until it eventually exploded in his big sex scandal of 2009?[26]

Unfortunately, children who have been parented according to this lie often grow up believing that contentment is found in pleasing others, since this was the pattern set for them as children. So when these children become adults, they end up pursuing work, relationships, and hobbies in order to earn favor, love, and acceptance from others—not necessarily because they are passionate or called to it. They will make decisions for the very same reasons—to please others. Other people's needs and wants—especially their parents'—will always come before theirs. And they will often "pursue careers that place them in the public eye—as politicians, athletes, or entertainers" because they're longing for the attention that their parents either constantly gave them, or never gave them.[27]

As Burgo was researching the deeper effects that narcissism and pride had on parenting, he also discovered another pattern among children who were raised by narcissistic parents. Many of them "grow up to be highly empathic individuals, well attuned to the wishes and wants of those around them. They make loyal friends and sympathetic listeners, with an ever-available shoulder and a willing ear."[28] As a result, many of them will often end up working in the helping professions, marrying a narcissistic spouse, or both.

Lest you mistakenly think that any of this should serve as positive justification to raising children in this manner, Burgo shares a stark and sobering reflection about his childhood with a narcissistic parent. "At an early age, I also sensed that my role in life was to redeem [my mother's] unhappiness through success."[29]

No one's purpose in life should be to redeem someone else's unhappiness—neither through success nor through any other means. That is not a way to live, and it applies a weight that no person can shoulder. Living vicariously through your children to fulfill your unfulfilled dreams is certainly no way to parent, either. Just consider the tragic legacy of Earl Woods—it's not Tiger's achievements, nor was it his ability to raise the world's greatest golfer. No, it's the fact that his family buried him in an unmarked grave somewhere in Kansas. What a slap in the face.

A Place to Start

It's hard to believe that I'm married and have three children. And every time my children celebrate a birthday—or those "On This Day" memories pop up on Facebook—I'm reminded of just how inadequate I felt *and still feel* about parenting. And this doesn't even include the number of times Christina and I have stared at each other in disbelief that we are actually responsible for the care, feeding, nurturing, and development of real live human beings.

Now after reading a chapter like this, it'd be easy to overcompensate and start psychoanalyzing every interaction you have with your children. "Why does she frustrate me more than the others? Why does he talk back? How does she know how to push my buttons? Was I too harsh? Why did I discipline him in that manner? Why am I pushing her toward this career path? Why am I so obsessed with his team winning? Why do I care so much? Why don't I care enough?"

While psychoanalyzing every jot or tittle of your *career* as a parent might be overkill and quite futile, a little dose of healthy self-reflection wouldn't hurt—especially if you believe you might have fallen prey to this lie that you are who you raise. This exercise will be particularly helpful considering the fact that we often parent according to our habits, routines, patterns, or *normals* of life. So here are a few questions to help you get started. Please don't read on until you've at least given them some thought.

- What childhood dreams have gone unfulfilled?
- What opportunities did you miss out on?

- What were you not allowed to do as a child?
- What upset you most about your parents?
- What is your fondest memory with your parents?
- What are the ways you've tried to live vicariously through your children?

As you worked through these questions, you probably cycled through a mix of emotions like shame, guilt, humiliation, embarrassment, fear, regret, surprise, hurt, or anger. You might've even discovered that the reason you parent the way you do is because you were parented in that same manner—or because you consciously decided to parent differently. All this is good, but to truly break free from this lie that you are who you raise, you have to start with forgiveness.

At a minimum, you need to forgive your parents for the way that they *unconsciously* wronged you. After all, they were probably just parenting the way that they were parented as well—without giving it much thought. And if you're serious about finding freedom from this lie, you must go a step further and forgive them for the ways that they *consciously* wronged you.

While I recognize that this might seem like a big ask, I'm not asking you to sweep everything under the carpet and act as if nothing happened. I'm not asking you to forget, nor do I expect that reconciliation will always take place—because it doesn't. I'm just asking you to start with forgiveness.

Forgiveness is something you can do regardless of the other party, whereas reconciliation requires both parties to do the hard work of repeatedly repairing and restoring trust over time. And unfortunately, you're not in control of how your parents will react, how long it will take, or if things will even ultimately change.

But here's what you are in control of: the first step. You can take the first step and begin walking the path toward freedom from this lie if you forgive. But don't just forgive—give it to Jesus instead. Invite Jesus into your hurt, shame, and guilt because he is "gentle and humble in heart" and he promises to help you find rest for your soul (Matt. 11:29 HCSB).

If you're courageous enough to forgive your parents—and invite Jesus into the process—here's what will happen. Jesus will take your hurt and shape it into healing. Over time, he will replace that stress with rest. And ultimately, he will break the chains that have been saddling you down with guilt and shame, so that you can begin living freely and fully. While reconciliation is not guaranteed on this side of eternity, at least you'll begin walking in freedom. I love the way that Jesus extends this invitation to us:

> "Are you tired? Worn out? Burned out on religion? Come to me. Get away with me

and you'll recover your life. I'll show you how to take a real rest. Walk with me and work with me—watch how I do it. Learn the unforced rhythms of grace. I won't lay anything heavy or ill-fitting on you. Keep company with me and you'll learn to live freely and lightly." (Matt. 11:28–30 The Message)

Conclusion

Whether it's helicopter parenting, lawn mower parenting, or whatever will come next—underneath it all is a desire for control. And if there's one empty promise the gig economy makes, it's control. In fact, do you remember that "creative control" was listed as one of the reasons children aspired to be YouTubers?

The only problem is that the older your children get, the less control you will have over them. So if your path to contentment is to live vicariously through your children, it will only work for so long. Eventually, when your children refuse to be controlled by you, and they cut you off or move away, what will you do then? Who or what will you turn to?

All throughout Tiger's life—even when he was in college—Earl controlled him. There was even one instance when Earl—being short on cash—*used* Tiger to put on a golf clinic. Earl barked orders, then Tiger hit the ball on command. Bark, hit, bark, hit. After doing this for forty-five minutes, Tiger faced the crowd and answered questions— actually, to be more precise, Earl answered for Tiger.

A child raised his hand and asked, "Tiger, what was your best score?" Earl answered the question. Another child raised his hand. "Tiger, what's your favorite club?" Earl answered again. A third child's hand shot up. "Yes," Earl said, acknowledging the boy. The boy pointed at Tiger and said, "Does he talk?"[30]

It's interesting to see what happened to Earl's controlling relationship with his son after Tiger turned pro. Instead of finding contentment—since the unfulfilled dreams that had been driving his life were finally realized—he continued to search for it. He thought that Tiger becoming the best golfer in the world would satisfy him, but it didn't. So in his quest for control and contentment—realizing that it's not found in who you raise—he turned to the lie that you are who you know. Instead of going to Tiger's tournaments and surrounding himself in his son's success, he surrounded himself with women instead. Rather than controlling his son—because he couldn't anymore—he switched his focus to controlling women by paying for them.

And that's the thing with this lie—and every other lie in this book. They seem so alluring because they give you the illusion of control—but they never keep their end of the bargain.

No matter what your children accomplish or achieve, it will never satisfy. Nothing they do will ever make you feel whole, fixed, or content. They will never be able to cover up the shame from your past, because you are not who you raise. So instead of trying to find contentment by controlling them, why not choose another way? These seven lies, including the one in the next chapter, just don't satisfy. They can't.

Chapter 7

The Other Side of Shame

Jobless, moneyless, homeless, and hopeless. Just fill in the blank, we were _____ less on April 1, 2010.

When we *abruptly* left Korea, everyone thought we were playing some April Fool's joke. And by *abruptly*, I mean selling *all* of our newly bought furniture, canceling our lease, dropping out of graduate school, and saying goodbye to our friends and coworkers, within three weeks, without telling them the real reason we were leaving Korea—and let's not forget that Christina and I also had a five-month-old child.

It was *that* shocking and surprising—both to us and to everyone else. Here are a few comments from Facebook to give you a sense into the abruptness of it all.

"Dude . . . you goin' somewhere?"

*"Nooooooo don't gooooo pastor daniel. it's
too early! :(where are u going, back to
Canada?"*

*"I need to know . . . WHERE ARE YOU
MOVING????"*

*"We'll miss you so much . . . :(Don't
leaveeeeeeee . . . I didn't even get to see
ur dog . . ."*

*"You mean you're stepping out all of a
sudden?"*

I found myself convincing others (or trying to convince myself) that it was planned, intentional, and strategic. I would say things like, "We wanted international experience!" Or I would give *rational* excuses like, "Now that we have a newborn, we felt like the wisest decision was to raise her back in Canada close to family."

But I'm sure people saw right through it. After all, things didn't add up. I was pastoring in a megachurch of fifty thousand people and leading a growing youth ministry. Both Christina and I were in the middle of our graduate degrees, we had just leased a new apartment and bought all new furniture, we had a newborn, and our community was incredible. So, of course, the logical thing would be to leave it all and *abruptly* move back to Canada to "discern our next steps," right?

For the sake of the church, we didn't want to leave guns blazing, even though everything within us was screaming to do otherwise. We wanted to defend ourselves, fight, and tell our side of the story, but we couldn't bring ourselves to do it because of the nasty aftermath that would result. The least they could do was pay for our plane tickets back to Canada. But no, they didn't even do that. All we got was a cold shoulder and a pink slip.

This was not the past that I wanted to start a family with. And I get that hardships are *supposed* to be good for you. After all, don't you grow through what you go through? Aren't struggles supposed to lead to strength? Don't you have to crack an egg before you can use it? And let's not forget that misattributed C. S. Lewis quote: "Hardships often prepare ordinary people for an extraordinary destiny."

I knew those clichés, and I certainly understood that there is a level of truth underneath them, but if you were in my shoes, how would you have felt if you had just lost your job, home, and sense of self-worth? And on top of that, if you had been told by your now-former boss that you weren't cut out to do what you're doing and should consider a career change? Wouldn't you want to run as far away from your past as possible?

As a husband and father, I felt like it was my responsibility to provide, so instead of dealing with the past, I compartmentalized it and immediately started handing out my résumé and applying for jobs. I wasn't ambitious, I just had to get a job—any job—and earn a steady income so that we could move out of my parents' house. As a grown man with a wife and baby, I was so embarrassed.

At first, I thought it'd be easy. I thought people would be busting down the doors trying to hire me because of my résumé and experience. But for months on end, there was nothing. Nothing but silence. Even for positions that I was *over*qualified for.

And I hated that—but it wasn't because of what this meant for my living arrangements. I hated it because in those moments of silence and waiting, the waves of shame and guilt would overwhelm me and fill my mind with thoughts like: *Because of your mistakes, you are now a mistake. You are the reason that you're not in Korea anymore. It's all your fault. And look who's suffering because of it. It's not only you, but everyone around you. Everyone.*

Rejection stings, doesn't it? And when applying for a job, silence *is* rejection. So how was I supposed to move on if there was nothing to move into? How was I supposed to figure out the future when I couldn't get my mind out of the past? Like a creepy stalker, the past wouldn't leave me alone—it just kept following me around. And when I would bury it, like the walking dead, it would just rise up and dig itself out of the ground. No matter how much I tried, or what I tried, compartmentalizing the past just didn't work.

Lie #7: You Are Your Past

What's interesting about the past is that it's not just made up of the things you've done. The things that others have done to you are often as important, if not more so, than the things you've done yourself. Reflecting on both will help you assess the extent to which the past affects your present.

So take a moment and answer the following questions about the things that you have done:

- What is one of your favorite experiences in life?
- What is an accomplishment that you are proud of?
- What are you ashamed of?
- What is a regret that you have in life?
- Which word best captures the essence of your Instagram, Facebook, or Twitter profile?

Now, take a moment and answer the following questions about the things that others have done to you:

- What is a memorable experience that someone did with you in your childhood?
- How did others encourage you after you accomplished something?
- When would others withhold love from you?
- While growing up, who or what were you afraid of?
- Which word best captures the essence of your childhood?

Do you see the past in your present? Do you see how the things that you've done, and the things that others have done to you, are still affecting you today? In your everyday life? If the answer is yes, and if working through those questions were uncomfortable or painful in any way, then congratulations! This lie that you are your past has latched onto you as well.

Compartmentalizing Is an Illusion

When we came back from Korea, I wanted that chapter of my life closed. I never wanted to reopen it again. So I did the very thing that I had decades of experience observing *and* doing—I compartmentalized it.

Growing up, I sat through a series of master classes on compartmentalization. My older sisters taught me how to compartmentalize conflict and hide my emotions. My dad taught me how to compartmentalize work from home. And my mom taught me how to compartmentalize my personal desires from what's best for the collective whole. If only compartmentalizing was a skill on LinkedIn. Tickets to "Daniel's Compartmentalizing Workshop" would be sold out for months! In fact, I've had so much experience compartmentalizing that I've learned how to switch off painful emotions and memories.

While that might seem impressive, especially since compartmentalizing is a must-have skill in the gig economy, the unfortunate (or fortunate) thing is that it never lasts— compartmentalizing is always temporary.

Health-care workers know what I'm talking about. For them, compartmentalizing seems to be a learned skill. After all, how else would you expect them to deal with the amount of grief, death, sickness, and trauma they encounter on a regular basis? So instead of debriefing and processing what happens, many of them simply push their emotions down or try and forget what happened through one means or another.

As common as this practice is, my oncologist friends, Julian and Chrissy Kim, who regularly deal with death and pain, don't see this as the only way. I love how they put it during one of our recent conversations:

Compartmentalizing painful truths and situations is akin to hitting the snooze button. It just kicks the problem of pain down the road. It ends up being a survival mechanism. The healthier thing to do is to debrief the cases and deal with reality, no matter how painful. If we don't do this, we'll lose our humanity and compassion and get bitter, cynical, or burnt out.[1]

As much as I tried to compartmentalize away everything that had happened in Korea, it kept on rearing its ugly head. I found myself hesitant to trust others because I didn't want to risk getting hurt. I also realized I was becoming reluctant to pray for others because I didn't want to be disappointed. And having hope that things were going to work out was absent because I didn't want to risk being let down. Until I fully faced and revisited what had happened, the past would just keep on coming up.

I love how Jean Vanier puts it. When we compartmentalize the past, we "let the hurt fester inside, creating an attitude of continual dis-ease and discontent with everything and everyone. The hurt that we hide can even turn into feelings of self-deprecation, as if we deserved it, because we have become convinced that we have no value."[2]

Compartmentalizing the past just doesn't work. It's like putting a Band-Aid on an infected cut without first treating it. You have the *illusion* of healing, while the problem just continues to spread underneath the surface.

Is Compartmentalizing Really a Skill?

Apparently, compartmentalizing is a skill. In fact, in the gig economy, it is a must-have skill. With popular articles on the Internet like, "11 Successful Women On How They Compartmentalize," "5 Steps of Compartmentalization: The Secret Behind Successful Entrepreneurs," and "How Productive People Compartmentalize to Get the Most Done," learning how to compartmentalize is now *easier* than ever.

Compartmentalizing is even one of the "6 Secrets to Your Survival in the Gig Economy," according to an article in *Inc.* magazine! No wonder compartmentalizing is getting so much press—it seems to be the only way to stay sane. Since juggling multiple jobs and believing the lie that we are what we do is normal in the gig economy, compartmentalizing has become *the way* to keep things separate. It's even been advocated as a way to increase productivity! So if you're working three jobs, the most productive thing to do is to have three identities that are separate and each in its own compartment . . . so goes the lie.

I recently came across an interesting study that was published in one of Cornell University's peer-reviewed journals in 2017. The researchers wanted to investigate the long-term effects of simultaneously working multiple jobs, and their findings were sobering. After gathering data for five years, they discovered that "people with multiple work identities struggle with being, feeling, and seeming authentic both to their contextualized work roles and to their broader work selves."[3] Put another way, working multiple jobs made the subjects feel like imposters. In at least one of their jobs, they would feel like they didn't belong and weren't qualified for the job, and that one day they were going to be found out.

Back in 1978, two researchers from Georgia State University stumbled upon the same thing when studying high-achieving women. They called it the Imposter Syndrome.[4] Now if you were to have told those two researchers that the Imposter Syndrome was going to become a cultural phenomenon forty-plus years later for both men and women, and that it was going to be connected to something that affects close to half of the workforce—the gig economy—I'm sure their reaction would've been priceless.

What's interesting about the Cornell research is just how many of the subjects found themselves believing the Imposter Syndrome *because* they worked multiple jobs. Here's how one of the subjects put it: "With multiple interests, a variety of passions, and a whole bunch of creative pursuits on the go, you're going to feel like a fraud sometimes. As if you've got it all wrong and that any day now you will be exposed as an outsider, as someone who doesn't know what they're doing."[5]

There's no doubt that compartmentalization, the gig economy, working multiple jobs, and Imposter Syndrome are all intertwined and feed into one another. What's confusing is trying to figure out which came first. It's like the age-old question of the chicken and the egg. And while we may never agree on the answer, it's fascinating how the research reveals that Imposter Syndrome is usually nurtured in us from a young age—albeit unintentionally and unconsciously—in one of two ways.

Did you ever feel like your parents played favorites? Did it ever seem like one of your siblings got more praise and attention than you—even when they didn't deserve it? And especially when you would come home with a great report card, first place in an athletic competition, or some other achievement you were proud of, did it ever feel like you could never impress your parents? If so, then Imposter Syndrome probably took root and grew deep inside of you, because every time this happened, you were essentially being told that you weren't good enough.

But what if you could never disappoint your parents? No matter what you did, you could do no wrong. And even if you came home with a bad grade on a test, your parents were always encouraging. If so, then Imposter Syndrome probably also took root in your heart because—at a deeper level—you knew that you weren't as good as your parents said you were. And even though your parents said it was okay, you were often disappointed in yourself.

If you feel like I'm reading your mail—in either instance—then you likely grew up with a sense of cognitive dissonance, which is actually the birthplace of Imposter Syndrome. You didn't know how to reconcile or explain the huge gap between the way you saw yourself and the way your parents saw you. You just knew that things didn't add up, and it was uncomfortable.

No wonder it's so easy to believe the lie that you are your past—just look at how deep it goes.

~~You Are Your Past~~

When it comes to the past, I have my regrets. I'm not quite sure where to begin, what to share, how much to share, if it's even necessary to share, or if I'll just later regret doing this all in the first place, but here we go anyway.

I regret running away from home as a teenager. I regret ditching my childhood friends for years to pursue a girl that I never even dated. I regret the years of pornography that I watched. I regret my abuse of alcohol and underage drinking. I regret lying to my parents over and over again. I regret cheating in school. I regret bullying others. I regret wasting thousands of dollars on frivolous things. I regret everything

I did with my ex-girlfriends before I got married. And I regret moving to Korea.

I've sometimes wondered if it was a mistake to go to Korea in the first place. It certainly was a great opportunity, but was it the right one? I wonder how much of the decision to go was led and influenced by my ego, pride, ambition, and drive to succeed and make a name for myself. I also wonder what would've happened if we didn't move to Korea. Would we have moved elsewhere? Or would we have just stayed in Montreal? And if we had just stayed in Montreal, I sometimes wonder what we would be doing right now, and *who* we would be.

In this day and age of fake news, half-truths are everywhere because they sound right—and that's precisely the reason they are so deceptive. They mingle truth and falsehood with the "deliberate intent to deceive."[6] Just consider the seven half-truths in this book: What you do for work affects how you see yourself. The things you experience shape your memories and perception of self. The people you know hold the power to shape you. What you know can either open or close doors. The things you own have a level of power over you. You are responsible for your children. And the past does affect how you see the world and approach it.

Do you see how these statements are true, but also incomplete at the same time? What you do, what you experience, who you know, what you know, what you own, who you raise, and your past all hold a critical role in the way that you see yourself, but they are not *the way* to see yourself because they all come up short. They're incomplete precisely because they're half-truths. This is why you can't let any of these lies become the primary lens through which you view yourself—especially the lie that you are your past, because it holds the potential to disable or destroy your future.

This lie will disable your future if you find yourself always wanting to relive the glory days, instead of seeing and stepping into what's next. There's a word to describe people like this: peaked. You know you've peaked if you find yourself constantly bringing up stories from high school or college when mingling at parties, if you're always shame-lessly posting pictures of your high school or college self on Throwback Thursday, and if your high school or college friends are your only friends. Underneath this behavior is the belief that your best days are behind you, which is why this lie is so successful at keeping people in the past. Unfortunately, believing the lie will not only keep you in the past, it will simultaneously disable you from stepping into the future.

This lie also has the potential to destroy your future if you find yourself filled with bitterness and unresolved hurt from the past. I'm not thinking of the kind of fringe individuals who have a hit list, or who are actively scratching people off their will (although, if that's you, I'd recommend getting some serious help). Rather, I'm referring to individuals who seem normal, for all intents and purposes, but who have muted or blocked friends on social media because of conflict. Or maybe you thought everything was fine, until you bumped into your ex or former coworker while getting coffee, and a flood of emotions derailed you for the day. Or perhaps it's just that you find yourself regularly saying things like, "I'll show you," or, "I deserved that," underneath your breath. If you said yes to any of these scenarios, or if you can envision similar ones, then the past has the potential to destroy your future.

All of these are telltale signs that this lie has a greater grip on you than you might have originally realized.

Beauty from the Ashes

There's a scene that's etched in my memory from the pilot episode of *The Man in the High Castle,* which is Amazon's dystopian "what-if" TV series. The context of this series is an America that's ruled by Nazi Germany and Imperial Japan because the Allies were defeated in World War II. The episode opens up in New York City, which is the regional capital of Nazi America. Twenty-seven-year-old Joe Blake, who seems to have been recruited for the Resistance, makes his way past Nazi agents, and into a shipping and moving company for his first assignment to "get his country back." His mission? To drive a package from the Greater Nazi Reich to the neutral zone in Cañon City, Colorado, which borders on the Japanese Pacific States.

While en route he blows a tire, and to his *delight*, a local Nazi police officer helps him repair it. Uncertain whether his undercover identity is going to be exposed, Joe nervously makes small talk with the police officer by pointing out something falling from the sky. It looks like snow, but it's not the right season for it, since all the trees are green and it's not even winter. Confused, he asks the officer, "What is that?" The officer looks up, and after noticing that it's ashes falling from the sky, responds nonchalantly, "Oh, it's the hospital. Tuesdays they burn cripples, the terminally ill . . . the drag on the state."

When you think about the word *ashes*, is this what comes to mind? Or is it the prayer, "ashes to ashes, dust to dust" that's common in funerals? Or maybe it's Linus's line in *It's a Mystery, Charlie Brown*: "Ashes to ashes and dust to dust, when there is a problem, in Snoopy we trust."

Technically speaking, ashes are the opposite of life. They represent the end, not the beginning. They are evidence of irreversible death and destruction. They are also a symbol of the past and a memorial of things that both helped and hurt. Just consider the aftermath of a campfire, a building that burns to the ground, or a body that's cremated. There's nothing you can do with the ashes. All practical functionality is gone and there's no chance of recovery—technically speaking.

However, when you look at the way that the word is used in the Bible, ashes represent more than just death and destruction. In Isaiah 61:3, "to give them a crown of beauty instead of ashes," seems to point to a deeper purpose for the ashes in our lives. It seems to suggest that ashes are not just a symbol of the past, but actually the path to the future. And instead of burying, scattering, or ignoring the ashes of your past, it seems to suggest that there's another option—the option of offering your past to Someone who has the power to create new life. Someone who holds the power to redeem, restore, and transform the ashes of your past into a crown of beauty.

Let's take a deeper look at the context surrounding Isaiah 61:3 to examine what would happen if we walked down this path.

> The Spirit of the Lord God is on me,
> because the Lord has anointed me
> to bring good news to the poor.
> He has sent me to heal the brokenhearted,
> to proclaim liberty to the captives
> and freedom to the prisoners;
> to proclaim the year of the Lord's favor,

and the day of our God's vengeance;
to comfort all who mourn,
to provide for those who mourn in Zion;
to give them a crown of beauty instead of
        ashes,
festive oil instead of mourning,
and splendid clothes instead of despair.
And they will be called righteous trees,
planted by the Lord
to glorify him. (Isa. 61:1–3)

What I love about the book of Isaiah is that it's part history and prophecy. If you were to read it, you would see the ways that God interacts with humanity, particularly when we turn our backs on him, as well as the ways that God is planning to save humanity through a Savior. You would see that God is not only the Creator, but that he is forgiving, merciful, just, and the great Redeemer as well. I love how Gordon Fee and Douglas Stuart put it: the book of Isaiah "gathers up the whole of the Old Testament story and prepares the way for the New."[7]

In passages like this one, the book of Isaiah is preparing the way for the New Testament by foreshadowing not only what is to come, but *who* is to come. And in this particular instance, the foreshadow is about a Savior who will, among many other things, replace the ashes we're sitting in with a crown of beauty—particularly for those who are hurting, brokenhearted, and captive to the lies of our age.

This Savior will not only heal our past, but will also redeem, restore, and replace our brokenness with beauty. I love what it says in another part of Isaiah:

> "Do not remember the past events,
> pay no attention to things of old.
> Look, I am about to do something new;
> even now it is coming. Do you not see it?
> Indeed, I will make a way in the
> wilderness,
> rivers in the desert." (Isa. 43:18–19)

You can't foreshadow unless you know what's going to happen; prophecies are empty unless they actually come true. So when more than three hundred prophecies about the coming Savior in the Old Testament came true in the birth, life, and death of Jesus Christ—including these two— everything changed.[8]

Just think about it for a moment. How could the Old Testament writers write together in such unison about Jesus when they died hundreds of years before he was born? And it's not like they developed some conspiracy—in most cases, they weren't even alive at the same time as one another. And how would they have been able to foreshadow and prophesy *that* accurately when they didn't know the future? Doesn't this point to divine intervention when the Old Testament was being written?

And seriously, to think for a moment that it was mere coincidence that all of these prophecies were fulfilled in a single individual is hogwash. Perhaps you could find one or two of them fulfilled in an individual, but not all of them! In fact, in Peter W. Stoner's book, *Science Speaks*, he outlines the mathematical probability of one person fulfilling just eight prophecies—just eight. Josh and Sean McDowell quote him in their book, *Evidence That Demands a Verdict*:

> We find that the chance that any man might have lived down to the present time and fulfilled all eight prophecies is 1 in 10^{17} (10 to the 17th power). That would be 1 in 100,000,000,000,000,000 (17 zeroes after the one).[9]

That's the probability of one person fulfilling just *eight* of the prophecies—yet how many more were actually fulfilled in Jesus! Heck, the odds of winning the lottery seem mighty good compared to the odds of one person fulfilling these Old Testament prophecies; when Mega Millions had a $1.6 billion jackpot in October 2018, the odds of winning it were a mere 1 in 302,575,350.[10]

Stoner even went on to calculate the probability of one person fulfilling forty-eight prophecies. I'll save you the explanation and just give you the number: it's 1 in 10^{157}. Just imagine what it is for three hundred prophecies! And lest you wonder whether or not the math was wrong, H. Harold Hartzler, PhD, of the American Scientific Affiliation, Goshen College, writes in the Foreword of Stoner's book:

> The manuscript for *Science Speaks* has been carefully reviewed by a committee of the American Scientific Affiliation members and by the Executive Council of the same group and has been found, in general, to be dependable and accurate in regard to the scientific material presented. The mathematical analysis included is based upon principles of probability which are thoroughly sound and Professor Stoner has applied these principles in a proper and convincing way."[11]

All of this matters because the prophecy we read about earlier, "to give them a crown of beauty instead of ashes" (Isa. 61:3), was fulfilled in, around, and through Jesus.

It was fulfilled *in* Jesus when he emerged from the ashes of death, after three days, and resurrected into new life.

It was fulfilled *around* Jesus when everyone around him went from mourning to joy after Jesus defeated sin and death by raising from the dead.

And it was fulfilled *through* Jesus—and still is—when we approach him in humility and offer him the ashes of our lives, rather than burying, scattering, ignoring, or compartmentalizing them. When we do this, Jesus promises to take the ashes of our past and transform them into a crown of beauty by redeeming, restoring, and healing us.

Conclusion

You are not what you do. You are not what you experience. You are not who you know. You are not what you know. You are not what you own. You are not who you raise. And you are definitely not your past.

There is a sense of freedom in knowing what and who you are not. But ridding yourself of these seven lies won't fill you—it'll just empty you. Unless you replace these lies with the truth of who you really are, you'll just find another set of lies—even stronger and more destructive—to replace these with.

This is why I love what Jesus says about truth and freedom: "Come to me, all of you who are weary and burdened, and I will give you rest. Take up my yoke and learn from me, because I am lowly and humble in heart, and you will find rest for your souls. For my yoke is easy and my burden is light" (Matt. 11:28–30). The path to freedom is through Jesus. The way to discover truth is through Jesus.

Living in chains to the seven lies of the gig economy is tiring. It's a grind and a hustle just to try and keep up. It's actually a fool's game because you will never feel caught up. However, if you decide to follow Jesus, he promises to set you free, because following him is a decision to follow the truth. It's a decision to walk out of darkness and into the light. He said it himself: "I am the way, the truth, and the life. No one comes to the Father except through me" (John 14:6), and "anyone who lives by the truth comes to the light" (John 3:21).

Freedom cannot be found in anyone else or through anything else—including and especially through these lies—because it's only through Jesus that you can experience true freedom. And here's the truth about freedom: "Truly I tell you, everyone who commits sin is a slave of sin. A slave does not remain in the household forever, but a son does remain forever. So if the Son sets you free, you really will be free" (John 8:34–36).

When you decide to lay down these seven lies—and any other foundation you have been building your life upon—and instead decide to follow Jesus, your status will change from slave to child. From enslaved to free. From no inheritance to full inheritance. From worker to heir. From being defined by what you do, what you experience, who you know, what you know, what you own, who you raise, and your past, to being defined by what Jesus has done for you. Essentially, from ashes to beauty.

Jesus is not asking you to fulfill a list of requirements before he will set you free from your past and the other lies in this book. That's what religion does. It tells you to do this, do that, pick yourself up, dust yourself off, wash your face, and get yourself right before you even have the chance for freedom. This is because religion and self-help tell you to *do*, whereas Jesus says *done*. Jesus has already fulfilled all the requirements for freedom on your behalf. All you have to do is come to him, admit you're broken and in need, and give him your life. Then and only then will you finally find rest from the hustle, grind, and go of the gig economy.

Epilogue

ast Christmas, when my brother-in-law suggested we play *Just Dance*, I wasn't quite sure what to expect. After all, was he going to be okay losing? Didn't he know that I used to breakdance? And how was everyone going to deal with my *mad skillz*?

So I decided to take it easy on him—and everyone else. I was going to restrict my movements and keep it simple. Instead of playing to win, I was going to approach the game as a coach and as an encourager to others.

Everything pretty much went as planned until "Uptown Funk," "Happy," and "Another One Bites the Dust" came on.

We all have songs like these, don't we? Ones that make our bodies move in ways that might embarrass those around us. And even if you look like Elaine from *Seinfeld* or Carlton from *The Fresh Prince of Bel-Air* when you dance, isn't there just something freeing about turning up the music and letting loose?

For the kids, it was the song, "The Fox (What Does the Fox Say?)." Although the first couple of times was fine, it eventually just sounded like "Baby Shark"—absolutely-annoying-how-did-this-get-so-popular-is-this-what-our-world-has-become ridiculous nonsense.

And then my parents joined in and brought it "Gangnam Style." Honestly, I couldn't believe it. They're typically so stoic, but I guess there's just something about music that makes even the most unlikely person move.

Have you ever wondered why? What is it about music that just makes us move? Why is it so universal—existing for millennia in every culture large and small?[1] And could it possibly be shaping us in subtle ways that we might not be aware of? Much like the seven lies of the gig economy?

It's Shaping You

If we're connected on Instagram, Twitter, or Facebook—it's @danielsangi on all of them—you've probably seen videos of my children dancing and singing. No, not like the von Trapp family—albeit, we have sung "Do-Re-Mi" on more than one occasion. It usually happens after dinner when we're playing a family game. Although I usually have music softly playing in the background, we have this tradition where the winner gets to choose the song that we all rock out and have a dance party to.

Well, this one particular evening after winning, I decided to go for a classic instead of choosing my customary victory anthem, "We Are the Champions" by Queen. I wanted to teach my kids the songs that I grew up on when I was their age, so I chose "A Whole New World" from Disney's *Aladdin*. It's embarrassing to admit, but when I was younger, my sisters and I went all out when we sang this song. We even role-played by acting out lines from the movie before we would do a full sing-along with the piano.

So there I was, belting out the lines from the song and encouraging my kids to sing along with me, until I started listening to what I was singing. Halfway through the chorus, there was this one particular line—that when it rolled off of my lips—immediately caused me to fumble around for my phone and hit "skip."

Have you read the lyrics recently? I can see why I loved the song as a child, but now as a parent, I've pretty much banned the song from my house. After all, what sort of parent would want their children living according to the garbage in this song anyway? To all of those lies? Probably the sort of parent who *loves* it when their children disobey them and run wild. And perhaps the sort of parent who *despises* the thought of their children learning patience, grit, and tenacity!

You might think I'm overexaggerating—and I might be to some extent—but frankly, it's hard to ignore all the research that continues to come out about music and the ways that it shapes us. And I'm not even talking about the unconscious ways that it does, since that's even harder to comprehend or recognize.

Just consider the fact that researchers have discovered a link between music and enhanced memory skills.[2] Perhaps this is why music therapy is now positively and effectively being used "as a way to treat neurological conditions such as Parkinson's and Alzheimer's disease, stroke, brain injury, anxiety, and depression."[3]

And have you seen the studies where researchers have discovered how music shapes our perception of touch, how we perceive others facial expressions, our level of creativity, and our ability to exercise harder and smarter by using energy more efficiently?[4] They've even seen, in some early studies, that music can make you more generous, empathetic, inclusive, and cooperative—depending on the lyrics and style of music.[5] And if that's true, it makes sense that music can probably do the opposite.

In other words, music is not neutral, just like the gig economy. Like music, the gig economy is all around us, shaping the way we approach work, life, and love in more ways than we might realize.

Thousands of Lies

Occasionally, Christina and I like playing *Two Truths and a Lie* with the guests that we interview on our podcast.

The trick is coming up with a lie that sounds like a truth—half-truths work equally as well.

What's interesting is that we've never had to share this advice with our guests because most of us have a bag of lies and half-truths that we've carried around our entire lives. In fact, don't you ever feel weighed down by them? It seems like everywhere we go, there they are—thousands of lies.[6] The magazines at the grocery store, the billboards on the highway, the commercials on TV, the ads on Facebook and YouTube, and the lyrics to the songs we hear are all trying to subversively shape our identity.

"If you looked the way she looked, more people would notice you."

"If you drove that kind of car, you would be respected."

"If your kids' clothes looked and smelled that clean, you would be a better parent."

"If you drink this, you will have more friends."

"If you vote this way, you will be endangering life as we know it."

While most of us can spot these lies in advertisements that we see and hear, it's harder to notice the lies and half-truths that are embedded in the songs that we listen to. No, I'm not talking about backmasking and subliminal messages in songs; I'm actually just referring to the lyrics in today's popular songs.

Just listen to the top songs on any billboard chart, and it won't take you long to begin hearing songs that both promote the seven lies of the gig economy, and others that counteract them. For example, "A Million Dreams" from the soundtrack *The Greatest Showman,* sounds positive, uplifting, and hopeful—what's wrong with that, right? Except for the fact that the lyrics are promoting the lie that you are what you do. In contrast, the lyrics from Hillsong's "Who You Say I Am" explain that you are not what you do because you are actually who God says you are—a loved child of God, who is not forsaken, but forgiven and chosen.

"Sober" by Demi Lovato is another great example of a musically brilliant song with questionable lyrics. Just read through the lyrics and you'll notice the lie that you are your past. Alternatively, "O Come to the Altar" by Elevation breaks down that lie with the truth that you can leave behind your hurts, regrets, brokenness, and mistakes, and instead trade them for joy when you walk into God's wide-open arms.

Around You and Everyone Else

The seven lies are not only around you; they're around everyone else too. They have subtly become the new normal.

So the next time you play the game "Two Truths and a Lie," which list will you pull your truths from? What about your lie? In other words, how do you see yourself?

Are you what you do? Or are you a child of God? (John 1:12)

Are you what you experience? Or are you a new creation? (2 Cor. 5:17)

Are you who you know? Or are you known by our loving Savior, Jesus? (John 10:27)

Are you what you know? Or are you complete in Jesus? (Col. 2:9–10)

Are you what you own? Or are you more valuable than silver or gold? (1 Pet. 1:18–19)

Are you who you raise? Or are you God's masterpiece? (Eph. 2:10)

Are you your past? Or are you free from all condemnation? (Rom. 8:1–2)

How do you think your life would be different if you lived according to the way God sees you? What would change?

As we've come to the end of this book, I can't think of any better way to wrap it up than with the famous words of the great philosopher Ace Ventura—aka Jim Carrey—"I think everybody should get rich and famous and do everything they ever dreamed of so they can see that it's not the answer."

Daniel Im

Notes

Introduction

1. "The Ascension of Cauliflower," https://www.nytimes.com/2018/06/08/well/cauliflower-vegetables-rice-pasta-carbs-gluten.html.
2. In 2017, "sales of products containing cauliflower as an ingredient grew 71 percent in dollars," https://www.nielsen.com/us/en/insights/news/2018/fad-or-fundamental-whats-next-for-health-wellness-in-2018.html.
3. https://www.edisonresearch.com/the-podcast-consumer-canada-2018 and https://www.edisonresearch.com/podcast-consumer-2018.
4. https://www.forbes.com/sites/louiscolumbus/2018/03/04/10-charts-that-will-change-your-perspective-of-amazon-primes-growth.
5. If you search "gig economy" in Google Trends, you'll see a sharp global spike in interest beginning July 2015 that's only continued to grow in the ensuing years.
6. "Freelancing in America: 2018," Upwork, October 2018, 18; https://www.slideshare.net/upwork/freelancing-in-america-2018-120288770/1.
7. These statistics are from the "Freelancing in America: 2018" study that Edelman Intelligence was commissioned to do by Upwork and Freelancers Union. This dataset is particularly valuable since they've been conducting this research since 2014. Gallup's "The Gig Economy and Alternative Work

Arrangements," is another helpful report on the overall trends of the gig economy in America.

8. Randstad's report "Workforce 2025: The Future of the World of Work," is a helpful study on the gig economy in Canada. Intuit and Emergent Research also conducted helpful research on the overall Canadian workforce. For the United Kingdom, see Kayte Jenkins', "Exploring the UK Freelance Workforce in 2016." For Australia, see Upwork's report, "Freelancing in Australia: 2015."

9. Seth Stephens-Davidowitz, *Everybody Lies: Big Data, New Data, and What the Internet Can Tell Us About Who We Really Are* (New York: HarperCollins Publishers, 2017).

10. https://health.howstuffworks.com/medicine/modern-treatments/leeches-in-modern-medicine.htm.

11. "So you've been bitten by a leech. What's the worst that could happen?," *Popular Science*, accessed June 10, 2018, https://www.popsci.com/so-youve-been-bitten-by-leech-whats-worst-that-could-happen.

Chapter 1: Hustle

1. https://blog.fiverr.com/the-year-of-do-it-starts-right-now/.
2. https://twitter.com/b_cavello/status/839876313473150976.
3. Timothy Keller, *Every Good Endeavor: Connecting Your Work to God's Work* (New York: Penguin Books, 2012), 107–8.

Chapter 2: Experiences > Things

1. Look up "Coke Friendly Twist" on YouTube to watch the commercial.
2. Bridget Murray Law, "Seared in Our Memories," last modified September 2011, http://www.apa.org/monitor/2011/09/memories.aspx.
3. Dan Goldman, Sophie Marchessou, and Warren Teichner, "Cashing in on the US Experience Economy," last modified December 2017, https://www.mckinsey.com/industries/private-equity-and-principal-investors/our-insights/cashing-in-on-the-us-experience-economy.

4. Ibid.

5. B. Joseph Pine II and James H. Gilmore, "Welcome to the Experience Economy," *Harvard Business Review*, July–August 1998, https://hbr.org/1998/07/welcome-to-the-experience -economy.

6. B. Joseph Pine II and James H. Gilmore, *The Experience Economy* (Boston: Harvard Business School Publishing, 2011), Kindle Edition Location 384–562.

7. Lee Hayhurst, "Survey highlights Instagram as key factor in destination choice among millennials," last modified May 24, 2017, http://www.travolution.com/articles/102216/survey -highlights-instagram-as-key-factor-in-destination-choice -among-millennials.

8. Denise Garcia, "Social media mavens wield 'influence,' and rake in big dollars," last modified August 13, 2017, https://www.cnbc.com/2017/08/11/social-media-influencers-rake-in -cash-become-a-billion-dollar-market.html.

9. Celie O'Neil-Hart and Howard Blumenstein, "Why YouTube stars are more influential than traditional celebrities," last modified July 2016, https://www.thinkwithgoogle.com/ consumer-insights/youtube-stars-influence.

10. H. B. Duran, "Why Women Turn to Social Media for Purchasing Decisions," last modified November 23, 2016, http://www.alistdaily.com/social/study-why-women-turn-to -social-media-for-purchasing-decisions.

11. Elle Hunt, "Instagram star Essena O'Neill: 'The way it all turned so negative just numbed me,'" last modified January 4, 2016, https://www.theguardian.com/media/2016/ jan/05/instagram-star-essena-oneill-the-way-it-all-turned-so -negative-just-numbed-me.

12. Suzanne Collins, *The Hunger Games Trilogy* (New York: Scholastic Press, 2008), Location 195, Kindle.

13. Ibid., Location 231.

14. Ibid., Location 195.

15. Ecclesiastes 4:4

16. https://www.youtube.com/watch?v=gmAbwTQvWX8.

Chapter 3: Me, Myself, and Maybe You

1. Aaron Smith and Monica Anderson, "5 facts about online dating," last modified February 29, 2016, http://www.pewresearch.org/fact-tank/2016/02/29/5-facts-about-online-dating.

2. Nancy Jo Sales, "Tinder and the Dawn of the 'Dating Apocalypse,'" last modified September 2015, https://www.vanityfair.com/culture/2015/08/tinder-hook-up-culture-end-of-dating.

3. Mike Ozanian, "How CrossFit Became a $4 Billion Brand," last modified February 25, 2015, https://www.forbes.com/sites/mikeozanian/2015/02/25/how-crossfit-became-a-4-billion-brand.

4. Andy Boxall, "Google Home too boring? You want Gatebox's cute virtual character in your life," last modified August 2, 2018, https://www.digitaltrends.com/mobile/gatebox-digital-human-smart-home-release-news.

5. Andy Boxall, "Take a hike, Alexa: Wendy's a beautiful digital human ready to be your friend," last modified February 28, 2018, https://www.digitaltrends.com/mobile/sk-telecom-reality-reflections-holobox.

6. Mark Penn, *Microtrends Squared* (New York: Simon & Schuster, 2018).

7. https://www.youtube.com/watch?v=K2JVj19HRaw.

8. Dave Itzkoff, "Excerpt: Inside the Final Days of Robin Williams," last modified May 8, 2018, https://www.vanityfair.com/hollywood/2018/05/robin-williams-death-biography-dave-itzkoff-excerpt.

9. Robert D. Putnam, *Bowling Alone: The Collapse and Revival of American Community* (New York: Simon & Schuster, 2000), 170.

10. Lee Rainie and Kathryn Zickuhr, "Americans' Views on Mobile Etiquette," *Pew Research Center*, August 2015, http://www.pewinternet.org/2015/08/26/americans-views-on-mobile-etiquette.

11. https://variety.com/2018/digital/news/smartphone-addiction-study-check-phones-52-times-daily-1203028454.

12. https://www.cnbc.com/2018/12/13/vitaminwater-offers-100000-to-stay-off-smartphones-for-a-year.html.

13. Ibid.

Chapter 4: The American Dream

1. https://www.forbes.com/sites/kurtbadenhausen/2017/03/29/introducing-the-forbes-american-dream-index-to-gauge-middle-class-prosperity.

2. Seth Godin, *Stop Stealing Dreams*, www.stopstealingdreams.com

3. http://www.startribune.com/how-the-recession-split-the-millennial-generation-into-haves-and-have-nots/422810293.

4. https://www.huffingtonpost.com/entry/college-costs-are-americas-cruel-graduation-gift_us_5af5bd48e4b032b10bfa4569?ncid=tweetlnkushpmg00000041.

5. https://www.monticello.org/site/jefferson/knowledge-power-quotation.

6. https://www.washingtonpost.com/opinions/how-nazis-destroyed-books-in-a-quest-to-destroy-european-culture/2017/02/24/244aee94-cdf3-11e6-a87f-b917067331bb_story.html.

7. https://berkleycenter.georgetown.edu/posts/the-violence-of-cambodia-s-past-threatens-educational-dreams-today.

8. Ibid.

9. https://www.nytimes.com/2013/04/23/health/donald-r-hopkins-how-to-eradicate-guinea-worm-disease.html.

10. https://www.cartercenter.org/health/guinea_worm/casetotals.html.

11. Joseph Grenny et al., *Influencer: The New Science of Leading Change, Second Edition* (New York: McGraw Hill Education, 2013), 71.

12. James S. Coleman et al., *Equality of Educational Opportunity* (Washington: U.S. Government Printing Office, 1966).

13. https://hub.jhu.edu/magazine/2016/winter/coleman-report-public-education.

14. http://time.com/longform/teacher-pay-salary-stories/.

15. https://www.washingtonpost.com/news/answer-sheet/wp/2013/12/05/nelson-mandelas-famous-quote-on-education.

16. https://www.ted.com/talks/ken_robinson_how_to_escape_education_s_death_valley/transcript.

17. https://www.forbes.com/sites/danschawbel/2018/01/03/adam-braun-how-hes-disrupting-the-education-system.

18. https://www.fastcompany.com/40489360/wework-founder-hopes-her-new-school-will-help-5-year-olds-pursue-their-lifes-purpose.

19. https://www.wegrow.com/curriculum.

20. https://en.wikipedia.org/wiki/Go_(game).

21. https://www.wired.com/2016/03/two-moves-alphago-lee-sedol-redefined-future.

22. https://www.techrepublic.com/article/ibm-watson-the-inside-story-of-how-the-jeopardy-winning-supercomputer-was-born-and-what-it-wants-to-do-next.

23. https://www.vanityfair.com/news/2017/03/elon-musk-billion-dollar-crusade-to-stop-ai-space-x.

Chapter 5: Hoarders "R" Us

1. https://www.aetv.com/shows/hoarders/season-8/episode-16/children-of-hoarders.

2. https://www.tlc.com/tv-shows/hoarding-buried-alive/videos/sweet-sixteen-nightmare.

3. https://www.tlc.com/tv-shows/hoarding-buried-alive/videos/buried-alive-who-sleeps-this-way.

4. https://www.tlc.com/tv-shows/hoarding-buried-alive/videos/buried-alive-living-in-the-front-yard.

5. https://tvbythenumbers.zap2it.com/cable/hoarders-has-best-a-premiere-ever-for-ae-with-adults-18-49/25002.

6. https://www.bostonglobe.com/magazine/2016/11/01/where-shows-get-wrong-hoarding/vnzaM9LsKM5P3HqGSrUteJ/story.html.

7. https://www.empireonline.com/movies/features/best-movies, https://www.rollingstone.com/movies/movie-lists/readers-poll-the-25-best-movies-of-the-1990s-20319/5-fight-club-229616.

8. Chuck Palahniuk and Jim Uhls, *Fight Club*, directed by David Fincher (Los Angeles: Fox 2000 Pictures, 1999).

9. Ibid.

10. Joshua Fields Millburn and Ryan Nicodemus, *Minimalism: A Documentary about the Important Things* (Catalyst, 2016).

11. Ibid.

12. The rule basically states that if you're off course by one degree, for every sixty nautical miles that you fly, you'll be one nautical mile away from your destination.

13. This story about Jack Whittaker is a compilation of three sources: https://www.washingtonpost.com/history/2018/10/24/jack-whittaker-powerball-lottery-winners-life-was-ruined-after-m-jackpot, https://abcnews.go.com/2020/powerball-winner-cursed/story?id=3012631, and https://www.youtube.com/watch?v=RPGzo6LkfuA&.

Chapter 6: It's Not about You

1. https://www.dailydot.com/upstream/elle-mills.

2. https://www.youtube.com/watch?v=zPm4rR1cmzU.

3. https://www.youtube.com/watch?v=FY81DRYLoac.

4. https://www.dailymail.co.uk/news/article-4532266/75-cent-children-want-YouTubers-vloggers.html.

5. https://www.telegraph.co.uk/education/2018/01/19/revealed-top-career-aspirations-todays-primary-school-children.

6. https://www.dailymail.co.uk/news/article-4532266/75-cent-children-want-YouTubers-vloggers.html.

7. https://www.nbcnews.com/business/business-news/youtube-career-or-college-new-question-facing-teens-n920581.

8. https://www.forbes.com/sites/natalierobehmed/2018/12/03/highest-paid-youtube-stars-2018-markiplier-jake-paul-pewdiepie-and-more.

9. https://www.nickpress.com/press-releases/2017/03/02/nickelodeon-signs-teen-sensation-jojo-siwa-to-overall-talent-deal.

10. https://www.youtube.com/yt/about/press, last accessed December 1, 2018.

11. https://www.fatherly.com/love-money/work-money/the-2017-imagination-report-what-kids-want-to-be-when-they-grow-up.

12.

13. Charles Duhigg, *The Power of Habit: Why We Do What We Do in Life and Business* (Doubleday Canada, 2012), Location 123.

14. Daniel Im, *No Silver Bullets: 5 Small Shifts That Will Transform Your Ministry* (Nashville: B&H Publishing Group, 2017), xv.

15. https://www.si.com/vault/1996/12/23/220709/the-chosen-tiger-woods-was-raised-to-believe-that-his-destiny-is-not-only-to-be-the-greatest-golfer-ever-but-also-to-change-the-world-will-the-pressures-of-celebrity-grind-him-down-first.

16. http://www.espn.com/espn/feature/story/_/id/22765432/tiger-woods-lebron-james-most-dominant-athletes-last-20-years.

17. https://www.forbes.com/sites/tonifitzgerald/2018/08/13/does-tiger-woods-still-boost-tv-ratings-make-that-a-resounding-yes.

18. Jeff Benedict and Armen Keteyian, *Tiger Woods* (New York: Simon and Schuster, 2018), Location 67.

19. Ibid., Location 276.

20. Ibid., Location 288.

21. Ibid., Location 418.

22. Ibid., Location 467.

23. Ibid., Location 428.

24. Joseph Burgo, *The Narcissist You Know: Defending Yourself Against Extreme Narcissists in an All-About-Me Age* (New York: Touchstone, 2015), 70.

25. Benedict and Keteyian, Location 761.

26. Ibid., Location 5831.

27. Burgo, 79.

28. Ibid., 78.

29. Ibid.

30. Benedict and Keteyian, Location 1692.

Chapter 7: The Other Side of Shame

1. On January 26, 2019 and February 11, 2019, we had a series of engaging conversations on Twitter about this topic. This quote is a compilation of Julian and Chrissy Kim's thoughts.

2. Jean Vanier, *Becoming Human* (Toronto: House of Anasi Press, 2003), 136.

3. Brianna Barker Caza, Sherry Moss, and Heather Vough, "From Synchronizing to Harmonizing: The Process of Authenticating Multiple Work Identities," *Administrative Science Quarterly* XX (2017), 1.

4. Pauline Rose Clance and Suzanne Imes, "The Imposter Phenomenon in High Achieving Women: Dynamics and Therapeutic Intervention," *Psychotherapy Theory, Research and Practice Volume 15, #3* (1978).

5. Ibid., 3.

6. *Merriam-Webster, s.v.* "Half-truth," accessed February 23, 2019, https://www.merriam-webster.com/dictionary/half-truth.

7. Gordon D. Fee and Douglas Stuart, *How to Read the Bible Book by Book: A Guided Tour* (Grand Rapids: Zondervan, 2002), 185.

8. Josh McDowell and Sean McDowell, *Evidence That Demands a Verdict: Life-Changing Truth for a Skeptical World* (Nashville: Thomas Nelson, 2017), 351.

9. Ibid., 231.

10. https://www.washingtonpost.com/business/2018/10/17/mega-millions-tweaked-odds-create-monster-jackpots-it-worked.

11. Peter W. Stoner, *Science Speaks* Online Edition (Chicago: Moody Press, 2002).

Epilogue

1. Steven Brown, Björn Merker, and Nils L. Wallin, *The Origins of Music* (Cambridge: The MIT Press, 2000), 3.

2. Ibid.

3. https://brainworldmagazine.com/music-rhythm-brain.

4. http://maxplanck.nautil.us/article/329/blame-it-on-the-bossa-nova-how-music-changes-our-perception-of-touch and https://www.fastcompany.com/3022942/the-surprising-science-behind-what-music-does-to-our-brains.

5. https://greatergood.berkeley.edu/article/item/five_ways_music_can_make_you_a_better_person.

6. http://www.nytimes.com/2007/01/15/business/media/15everywhere.html.

— ALSO BY DANIEL IM —

No Silver Bullets explores five micro-shifts that have the potential to produce macro-changes in your church.

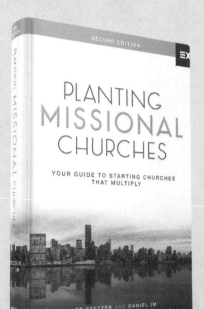

In this second edition of *Planting Missional Churches* by Ed Stetzer and Daniel Im, you will find a completely redesigned book with new content in every single chapter.

You will also find several new chapters on topics such as church multiplication, residencies, multi-ethnic ministry, multisite, denominations and networks, and spiritual leadership.

ABOUT
DANIEL IM

Daniel Im is a speaker and leader who has traveled to cities like New York, Vancouver, Los Angeles, Sydney, and Seoul to teach, consult, and coach. His podcasts have been downloaded over 3 million times. He has pastored in five major cities around the world in churches ranging from 100 people to 50,000 people. He has written two paradigm shifting books, *No Silver Bullets: Five Small Shifts that will Transform Your Ministry*, and *Planting Missional Churches: Your Guide to Starting Churches that Multiply* (second edition). He has an MA in Global Leadership and is a Gallup Certified Strengths Performance Coach. After several years of coaching and consulting leaders with LifeWay, Daniel and his wife, Christina, relocated back to Canada with their three children. As a pastor, he now brings executive leadership to Beulah Alliance Church in Edmonton, Alberta.

For more information about Daniel and how to bring him to your event, visit **danielim.com**.

For more information about the book, visit: **danielim.com/youare**